Peer Coaching
for
ADOLESCENT
WRITERS

Jeff—

Happy Peer Coaching !!

Susan

I dedicate this book to my third-grade teacher Miss Niblack (now Mrs. Nancy Stockmaster). Like most of my student writers, there was a teacher behind my inspiration, someone who respected my writing in its eight-year-old form—with misspellings and improper (albeit emerging) usage. She read beneath those surface metaphors and helped me realize this dream of becoming a writer and of all the doors that would open as a result of it. As she allowed me to read my stories aloud to the class and get feedback from my peers, writing became my cherished friend. The impact of those teaching actions that came so naturally to her as a new teacher were far-reaching indeed, and they reach farther now as a result of this book. A deep thank you, Miss Niblack.

Peer Coaching
for
ADOLESCENT
WRITERS

Susan
Ruckdeschel

Foreword by
Diane E. DeFord

CORWIN
A SAGE Company

Photos on the cover and on pages 3, 14, 20, 37, and 71 copyright © 2009 by Kate Rivera; photo on page 28 copyright © 2009 by Lex Filipowski; photo on page 58 copyright © 2009 by Misael Mora.

For information:

Corwin
A SAGE Company
2455 Teller Road
Thousand Oaks, California 91320
(800) 233-9936
Fax: (800) 417-2466
www.corwinpress.com

SAGE India Pvt. Ltd.
B 1/I 1 Mohan Cooperative Industrial Area
Mathura Road, New Delhi 110 044
India

SAGE Ltd.
1 Oliver's Yard
55 City Road
London EC1Y 1SP
United Kingdom

SAGE Asia-Pacific Pte. Ltd.
33 Pekin Street #02-01
Far East Square
Singapore 048763

Printed in the United States of America.

Library of Congress Cataloging-in-Publication Data

Ruckdeschel, Susan.
Peer coaching for adolescent writers / Susan Ruckdeschel; foreword by Diane E. DeFord.
    p. cm.
Includes bibliographical references and index.
ISBN 978-1-4129-7388-5 (cloth : alk. paper)
ISBN 978-1-4129-7389-2 (pbk. : alk. paper)
    1. English language—Composition and exercises—Study and teaching (Middle school)
2. English language—Composition and exercises—Study and teaching (Secondary)
3. Peer-group tutoring of students. I. Title.

LB1631.R835 2010
808′.0420712—dc22   2009023357

This book is printed on acid-free paper.

09 10 11 12 13 10 9 8 7 6 5 4 3 2 1

Acquisitions Editor:	Carol Chambers Collins
Editorial Assistant:	Brett Ory
Production Editor:	Cassandra Margaret Seibel
Copy Editor:	Adam Dunham
Typesetter:	C&M Digitals (P) Ltd.
Proofreader:	Scott Oney
Indexer:	Sheila Bodell
Cover Designer:	Karine Hovsepian

Contents

List of Figures

Foreword

Peer Coaching for Adolescent Writers outlines an easy-to-implement writing program for adolescent writers and their teachers in middle and high school settings. Susan Ruckdeschel gives practical guidance to teachers and students alike based upon her years of experience as a writer and teacher of writing. For classroom teachers, Susan's book provides the necessary guidance to ensure a seamless, well-conceived writing program. For students, it offers a nurturing approach to their emerging craft as writers, and demonstrates how to listen and respond constructively to their peers.

With many layers of support for teachers and students, each chapter addresses different aspects of planning, implementing, evaluating, and managing a writing program for adolescent writers as peer coaches. The student roles in the peer coaching process—writer, responder, manager and editor—are described in detail, and teachers are provided with advice on how to gauge student readiness for each of these different roles, as well as with lessons to scaffold students' learning within and across roles. Whatever the tools writers or teachers need, Susan has anticipated the need. *Peer Coaching for Adolescent Writers* offers sound methods, detailed guidance, and user-friendly assessments that guarantee successful, effective writers.

As a writer, I resonated with several themes within this text. First, the writer is at the center of this coaching model. The writer's goals for their own writing, the issues they face, the questions they have, and the feedback they want initiate each coaching event. Second, the process honors the fact that writers' goals may change as they write their way to deeper understanding of their own intentions. Finally, the coaching round ends with the writer, too. Decisions about what feedback the writer wants to incorporate rest in the writer's hands. For writers to realize the power of their own words, the final word must be theirs! However, writers need other writers, too. The writing community is used effectively to promote the writer's craft. This social connectedness of each writer to other writers seems to be the primary goal of this model.

As a coach (of readers, writers, and teachers), I loved that in Susan's model the first responsibility the coach has is to *listen.* The response the coach makes is to the writer, tailored to the writer's goals, issues, and requests for feedback. I do find that this responsive stance is hard to learn, and so I appreciated the guidance she provides to students so that they can learn to listen and respond to the writing of others in a supportive way. There are checklists, forms, and protocols that aid students and guide their responses to the writing of others. The rubrics Susan includes in the text will help the coaches monitor their own growth in providing feedback. One side of coaching is dealing with the fear others may have in receiving feedback or sharing their writing, for example. Susan effectively addresses this and other issues that can affect writers and their writing. One unique option is "silent" peer coaching, an option that allows for distance coaching or for application to settings other than traditional classroom venues.

As a teacher, I found the lessons, rubrics, and support materials (forms, transcripts, posters, and step-by-step procedures and protocols) to be very helpful. The directions provided so that writers, responders, managers, and editors can learn to be effective in each role were thorough as well as practical. The processes outlined within this volume are dedicated to building a strong writing community, and to increasing student responsibility, ownership and collaboration. I think teachers will also appreciate the connections to writing in other content area subjects, national standards, and adaptations for students with special needs and English language learners. The expertise that Susan brings to this topic will make this book popular with many different populations of writers, teachers, and other professional developers.

Diane E. DeFord
Swearingen Literacy Chair
University of South Carolina

Acknowledgments

A big "thank you" to two Carols simultaneously: Carol Collins, my editor at Corwin Press, for her faith in this project from the onset. That initial phone call from a very busy desk with other phones ringing in the background led to some creative, collaborative thought, and then a brainswell of ideas later: *Peer Coaching for Adolescent Writers*. Then Carol Poole, a very needed life raft as I lay afloat in a sea of words and many good ideas, but a teacher without a life raft is only as good as her students without a teacher; we needed each other! Carol Poole was my peer coach, and over numerous buddy sessions, she assisted with and contributed to the many ideas that make this book so teacher-friendly. Sometimes, peer feedback is brutal, often sending us back to the writing table, but we are always better for it in the end—especially our writing. I thank both Carols for their (occasionally brutal) honesty and for allowing me to revisit the writing table again and again. This book is better for it.

I would also like to thank all of the young writers that influenced me throughout my teaching career and that continue to teach and inspire the writer I will always be: my daughter, Miranda (her poem "I Can Hear the Leaves"); and Kate Moynihan in particular, for her unwavering dedication to the written word. It is this influence that informs my every next step regarding this book, future books, and what I know about how writing works for adolescent writers and about how it worked for me. Not a lot has changed; our pens and keyboards, creative ideas, a few coaching buddies, someone to believe in us—all simple ingredients to those writing life constants. To my students: Keep writing!

PUBLISHER'S ACKNOWLEDGMENTS

Corwin gratefully acknowledges the contributions of the following reviewers:

Diane Barone, Foundation Professor of Literacy Studies, University of Nevada, Reno, Reno, NV

Marsha D. Baumeister, PhD, Assistant Professor, Street, MD

Tracy Taylor Callard, English Language Arts Teacher, Wichita Public Schools (Hadley Middle School), Wichita, KS

David Callaway, 8th-Grade Language Arts Teacher, Highlands Ranch, CO

Dr. Barbara Smith Chalou, Professor, University of Maine at Presque Isle, Presque Isle, ME

Carrice Cummins, Associate Professor, Louisiana Tech University, Ruston, LA

Pamela F. Summers, EdD, Associate Professor, Literacy Department, SUNY Cortland, Cortland, NY

About the Author

 **Susan Ruckdeschel** graduated from Nazareth College of Rochester in 1991 with a master's of science in education. As a reading specialist, Susan taught, directed, and pioneered many school and district writing initiatives, beginning in 1991 in the Naples Jr./Sr. High School in the Finger Lakes Region of New York State. The student peer coaching model used in this book quickly expanded to other districts both inside and outside of classroom instruction to include the Glens Falls Middle School in Glens Falls, NY; the Booker T. Washington High School in Norfolk, VA; and the Hawthorne PEARLS School in Yonkers, NY. Student peer coaching continues to grow into regional and national popularity while Susan provides student peer coaching workshops for teachers and students.

Susan is working toward completion of a doctoral degree in literacy. She continues to work as writing consultant and instructor of reading methods and content literacy for schools and universities throughout the country, to include the University of Phoenix and Ashford University. She holds several NYS teaching certifications including Reading K–12, English 7–12, Classroom N–6, School District Administrator, and Gifted and Talented Extension. Susan has taught within each of these certification areas during her many years of teaching and consulting in public schools, as well as for organizations including the National Urban Alliance and the Pearson Learning Group. As founder of Literacy Solutions, Susan consults in districts throughout the country on curriculum and professional development. For updates on materials (lessons and other resources) related to this book, go to www.studentpeercoaching.com.

Introduction

Helping Adolescents Take Responsibility for Their Writing

> What hasn't changed since 1973 are adolescents themselves. They still crave meaning . . . They still want their writing and reading to matter to them and to matter now, not in some nebulous someday.
>
> —Nancy Atwell, Afterword in *Adolescent Literacy: Turning Promise Into Practice*

Long before I became a teacher, I was a writer. And, like many adult writers I know, writing saved my life. Writing—not a club, or involvement in a school newspaper, or even a specific teacher—but the fact that I wrote, wrote regularly, and exercised the art of my own expression. And like many kids today, my life as a child contained some unique, and some not-so-unique, challenges. While my friends were sneaking out of their bedroom windows and hanging out in shopping plazas (we didn't have Digg, Facebook, Flickr, Twitter, DandyID, or any type of Web presence then), I wrote. When nothing made sense about the world, my writing did as I typed away on my old Smith Corona, the noise and clatter drowned out by heavy keystroke and thought—my first poem was written at the age of eight and titled, *The Stranger I Once Knew* (my mother). My writing *was* my salvation.

WRITERS NEED OTHER WRITERS TO MAKE THEIR WRITING BETTER

Along my path to the writing life, I quickly discovered that writing in isolation only worked to the extent that a piece of writing was produced. I needed my writing to be heard and validated in order to move it forward; I needed to hear what other writers wrote about and what they thought about my work—we needed each other. As an adult, I sought out feedback through writing groups—evening coffeehouse meetings with other writers, all coming together to coach and support one another unconditionally in our writing effort. As a new teacher, I quickly realized that there was really only one difference in the knowledge and effort adult writers brought to their writing and what students brought to peer coaching in the classroom: That difference was in the pedagogy needed to get them from Point A to Point B; the steps to be taken along the way.

Simply put, writers need other writers in order to really make their writing better, especially our 21st-century adolescent writers who now take advantage of highly technological tools to communicate with each other expediently, regularly, and conveniently. Indeed, our teens seem to be hardwired for instant communication, and certainly they have readily available media to accommodate them—far more than we had as kids. While their *means* of communication have changed, their *need* to communicate hasn't. What is more, they still want to matter, and they still want what they do to matter in an immediate sense (Atwell, 2007).

What must change is not students' need to communicate nor their desire to matter; rather, the change must come in the *methods* we as teachers of writing use to teach them to respond to each other's needs. Those of us who think and write seriously about the craft of writing have been expressing that need for change since the sixties, demonstrating it through numerous models—student conferencing, peer feedback, peer review—all of them taught for decades as effective writing practice beginning with the introduction of Murray's (1985) process writing models, then moving on to Elbow's (1973) Center of Gravity method and teacherless writing groups. Shortly after, Graves (1983) gave us writing with purpose and peer-response groups. That same year, Lucy Calkins (1983) worked with peer conferences, and 15 years later, Nancy Atwell's (1998) reading and writing workshops developed the ideas further. Her work led us to Fletcher and Portalupi's (2001) Author's Chair and response groups, and three years after that, Kirby, Kirby, and Liner's (2004) self-evaluation writing processes added their input into the process. This review contains only a few examples of the literature focused on peer review functioning as a tool in the teaching of the writing craft to adolescent writers, always emphasizing that writers need other writers to make their writing better.

Student peer coaching is a means, an interactive process adolescent writers use to develop an internal, permanent, and intuitive dialogue for reviewing and editing their work through the use of a three-step intensive review process. Using specific protocols throughout each step, students of *peer coaching* establish writing goals, articulate needs, listen actively, and give and take feedback to employ a method of communication and decision making that leads to the production of polished, finished writing products. The student peer-coaching protocols are rooted in what research says, and has always said, about process writing, high-stakes writing demands, and the need for peer feedback when editing one's own work. Research has shown that development and practice with peer coaching or similar methods results in better performance when writing independently, especially when writing on demand for high-stakes assessments.

ADOLESCENT WRITERS AND THE NEED TO TEACH PEER FEEDBACK EXPLICITLY

The need for adolescents to talk and interact with each other has never been greater, and their enthusiasm for communication has never ceased—not in the sixties, nor the seventies, and certainly not now as facilitated by the technologies they interact with daily and that are growing by the minute—Live Spaces, Facebook, Bebo, MOG, Twitter, Loopt, YouTube, Friendster, Safebook, IMing, blogging, and whatever else becomes the latest adolescent social networking platform. While these venues allow students to express themselves, they aren't formal and often lead to nothing more than social chatter, or empty discourse, requiring nothing close to the oral or written skills necessary for high school graduation and beyond.

To move student writing forward, students need to be taught what to write and how to write it. *We* need to do that. Taking adolescents through a process that shows them how to respond to one another's writing—what they need, what to look for, what to listen for, how to phrase feedback—provides them with interactive skills to make the more formal discourse work *for* them. Because talk is the most natural thing we do (Beers, Probst, & Rief, 2007), and certainly that our adolescents do, we therefore need to teach them how to talk about their writing, so it too becomes a natural process. As their teachers, we therefore need to show them the steps to reach these goals; we need to teach them explicitly and emphatically how to arrive there.

THE NEED TO LISTEN EXPLICITLY

While writing is the heartbeat of student peer coaching, listening is the valve that keeps the blood circulating and the words flowing. An adolescent's ability to listen effectively flows from the nerve center in the brain that houses all feedback response, informing listeners what to respond with and writers what to do next. With training, students master listening actively and with intention for what writers have stated they need. Donald Graves (1994) says that when students can listen to themselves, they become reflective; he goes on to emphasize that the conditions we teachers set up in our classrooms, and through our instruction, are pivotal to the development of student listening abilities. When adolescent writers are able to shift back and forth between listening and reflecting, they become effective responders of important feedback, developing a 21st-century skill crucial to moving forward in life outside of our classrooms.

HIGH-STAKES ASSESSMENT
PERFORMANCE AND STUDENT PEER REVIEW

Welcome to the world of high-stakes assessments. Never before in our nation's history have students, teachers, and administrators been held so accountable for academic performance. So accountable, in fact, that federal and state funding, enrollment, and graduation hinge upon the result of performance assessments. High-stakes writing tests expect students to perform, in a window of time usually no longer than 20 minutes, a writing task that could take up to a week under normal circumstances. *And* they are expected to be successful. *Or else.* Unless they've internalized a dialogue that will advance their writing, they are alone in this effort, without an internal mechanism to inform them. Outside of the assessment venue, they may have lots of resources: teachers, peers, organizers, checklists, rubrics, models of good writing, and generic variations of student peer coaching, but can they transition from these resources to a write-on-demand session of 10 to 20 minutes? Making that transition is a significant result of any peer-review effort.

Recent research suggests strong ties between process writing, peer-feedback practices, and increased student performance on high-stakes assessments. Studies have shown that the internal dialogue and application of the intrinsic process for writing, resulting from peer-feedback instruction, is crucial to developing independent writers (Hawe, Dixon, & Watson, 2008; Moran & Greenberg, 2008; Simmons, 2003).

In the Moran and Greenberg (2008) study, students were trained to become what they called "Meta-Editors" (or peer editors). The position was taken that unless time was built into the class day for the teaching of structured feedback, students were unlikely to transfer revision or editing strategies when writing on demand. At the end of the study, interviewed students felt more confident about their ability to edit and screen for useful rather than less useful feedback. Not only did they express greater confidence in their writing ability; these students scored in the accelerated range on the 2007 Ohio Graduation Tests (OGT's), demonstrating the extent of growth of their writing skills. A similar study coming out of New Zealand (Hawe, Dixon, & Watson, 2008) was instrumental in producing a National Assessment Strategy which offers specific directives for assessing students in their use of targeted feedback, goal setting, peer and self-assessment.

Another very important study, by Simmons (2003), considered high school students across a range of socioeconomic and geographic variables (urban, suburban, rural) over a three-year period in their use of peer feedback. The study proved conclusively that the students, all college bound, needed considerable practice in models of peer review that exceeded the traditional semester or even yearlong writing course, and that they wrote better when using peer feedback that taught them to look for and respond to more than grammar and usage. While one group of students edited and revised according to written teacher comments, the other was taught specific models of peer feedback, including substantial commenting on content, or "strategies of readers and writers" (Simmons, 2003, p. 689). As with the previous studies, students who received feedback training felt their writing improved and that they had become better writers. In addition, the high school students who used peer feedback averaged more than 6 on a 2 to 8 grading scale. Students revising with only teacher comments scored lower, at 5.67. This study determined that

> the most academically talented students don't necessarily make the best reviewers of their peers' writing. Students need to practice reading one another's work while giving and receiving feedback before they do more than edit or offer global praise . . . they write better when using peer feedback and attending to the effects of their writing on readers and themselves. (p. 684)

As shown in the above studies, research continues to demonstrate that when adolescent writers respond to their peers with a focus on meaning and substance, including needs and goals rather than usage and grammar, writing skill advances significantly and quickly. In addition to improving writing skill, adolescents take ownership of, and responsibility for, their writing through goal setting, trouble shooting, listening actively, and giving and taking feedback—crucial undertakings for any peer-review effort.

NAVIGATING THIS BOOK

This book is designed to be a complete resource for full classroom implementation of all aspects of student peer coaching. Part I is devoted to the theory and research support for student peer coaching in Grades 6 through 12, offering insight on the needs of adolescent writers, along with the author's experiences as a young writer. Important studies on models of student feedback as they apply to high stakes performance and state assessments are integrated with insight on the need to explicitly teach peer feedback. Chapter 1 is comprised of the "how tos" for understanding and teaching the roles, steps, and protocols students must use to effectively employ the student peer-coaching methods in this book. Included are descriptions of the four student roles, the three steps with their protocols, model lessons, and tools for implementation. Chapter 2 describes two alternative peer-coaching methods: *silent peer coaching* and *peer coaching as questioning.* Chapter 3 outlines the important process of scaffolding responsibility to students, and Chapter 4 provides direction in facilitating and evaluating all of this effort for teachers as well as adolescent writers. In Part II, Chapters 5 through 7 get into the nuts and bolts of student peer coaching, beginning with Step One in Chapter 5, Step Two in Chapter 6, and ending with Step Three in Chapter 7. Included in these chapters are specific instructions on executing each step in the two most pivotal roles: writer and responder. Each of these chapters closes with a series of lessons geared toward teaching students the skills they need to become masterful peer coaches. Finally, Part III contains all the reproducible resources—checklists, organizers, rubrics, and posters teachers and students need for implementing each step and each protocol within the steps. Rubrics for teacher evaluation of students, peer self-evaluation, and peer-to-peer evaluation are included for implementing an ongoing, informal assessment. Each time one or more of the forms in Part III are referenced in the text, you will see this icon in the margin.

Approach this book as you would any new reading task: Preview the table of contents, the list of reproducible classroom resources in Part III, the charts and graphs, and even the model lesson plans in Chapters 5, 6, and 7. Then, read with an open mind and heart, from beginning to end.

Like all the teachers before me who have nurtured writers, including Miss Niblack to whom I dedicate this book, and all the authors of writing craft who have given and continue to give us more reasons to believe in our students, my hope—my dream, my wish—is that the student peer-coaching process in this book will help to nurture a community of writers in your classrooms. Happy peer coaching!

PART I

The Model

MASTER MATRIX OF STUDENT ROLES

ROLE: Writer

Step One:

Establish goals and issues, and make a feedback choice.

- Communicate your goal for the writing.
- Decide what issues you need help with.
- Select a type of feedback:
  1. Feedback on goals only
  2. Feedback on issues only
  3. Feedback on goals and issues
  4. "I heard . . ." feedback only
  5. No feedback (only available once)

Step Two:

Summarize and read.

- Summarize your writing in one minute or less.
- Read your piece aloud to the responder.

Step Three:

Decide what feedback to use.

- Take what you need (in feedback), and leave out what you do not.
- Make adjustments to your writing.

ROLE: Responder

Step One:

Listen for the goals and issues.

- Listen carefully for what the writer says his or her *goal* is for the writing piece (take notes, ask questions).
- Listen carefully for what the writer says she or he *needs* help with in feedback, or the issues. Ask clarifying questions when necessary.

Step Two:

Listen to the piece as it is read (listening with a purpose).

- Listen to provide feedback.
- Employ active listening.

Step Three:

Give feedback to the writer.

- First, say what you liked best using "I liked . . ." followed by "I heard . . ." statements.
- Next, offer feedback focused on what the writer asked for.
- *Do not* use the word *you* in a statement unless it is a question or in an "I liked . . ." phrase.

ROLE: Editor

Responsibilities:

- Provide helpful feedback to the writer before and after peer-coaching sessions.
- Use one of the editor's checklists when helping the writer:
  o Editor's Before Coaching Checklist
  o Editor's After and Between Coaching Checklist
  o Editor's Final Coaching Checklist
- Keep track of the writer's goals and issues; offer help where needed.
- Keep track of the feedback the writer asks for.
- Help the writer use his or her feedback.
- Provide the writer with helpful feedback for editing her or his piece.

ROLE: Manager

Responsibilities:

- Help organize and keep track of peer-coaching sessions.
- Use the Manager's Checklist to coach and help the writer, responder, and editor in fulfilling their roles.
- Use statements such as "I liked . . ." and "I might . . ." when making suggestions to peers.
- Offer assistance to participants as needed in fulfilling their roles successfully; include use of the proper forms and checklists.

Student Roles and Steps of Peer Coaching

What They Look Like in the Classroom

> *Since I can't possibly attend to the needs of 24 students, it's crucial that I*
> *teach students how to support one another and themselves.*
> —Laura Robb, *Easy-to-Manage Reading & Writing Conferences*

Four student roles drive the coaching effort. Two are absolutes: *writer* and *responder.* Two other roles—*editor* and *manager*—operate more flexibly and are worked in when students fully understand the writer and responder roles.

ROLES AND STEPS IN A NUTSHELL

The matrix at the start of Part I, placed there for ease of reference throughout your perusal of this book, outlines the steps and protocols for the pivotal tasks of each of the student peer-coaching roles: writer, responder, editor, and manager. Students will come to know these role tasks well. Note that it is important for reinforcement to use consistent language when referencing all program steps and protocols. Hanging the posters found in Part III (Nos. 31–36) around the classroom so that they are always visible will help to reinforce the steps while serving as a regular reference point for students as they assimilate the process.

As you can see from the Master Matrix on page 2, within each step of student peer coaching there are specific communication protocols to follow, such as (1) how to begin a feedback statement, first with "I liked . . . ," then with "I heard . . . ," thus avoiding *you* statements unless in the form of a question or *I liked* phrase; (2) how to verbally position a goal in front of peers with "I need . . . "; and (3) how to listen effectively and intentionally using organizers, checklists, and notes. Ultimately, student writers apply an intentional think-through process to decide what feedback to use and what feedback not to use in their writing effort while drawing on the peer-coaching process to respond with the appropriate feedback.

Here are a few field-based principles on the whys of the student peer coaching steps—basics keyed to my work in the field with student writers and the pedagogy I continue to apply:

- Students (especially adolescents), however well meaning or *not* so well meaning, need direction in responding to peers both in and out of the classroom. Not always effective in how they respond, they can lapse easily and quickly into negative discursive environments or simply say the wrong thing at the wrong time. Students need to be focused on the reader and his or her stated needs and goals in order to be supportive enough to offer effective feedback—this is teamwork.

- Students respond to themselves and to each other better when they set goals for their writing; their goals should be specific to each writing piece and to the writers themselves, as well as to the teacher's parameters for the project. Goal setting helps students identify and pay attention to areas that need focus in order to fully develop their writing and problem solve where needed.

- Adolescent students respond to each other more effectively when taught the appropriate language to use. When they *all* use that language, the playing field is leveled, a safety net is provided, and their need for structure is met. Middle and secondary school students need to know that there are rules in place that keep language appropriate, positive, and flowing.

THE CLASSROOM MODELS
WHOLE CLASS, GROUPS, BUDDIES

When teaching peer coaching for the first time, it makes best *logistical* sense to teach it as a whole class activity—students can see it modeled, ask questions that elicit answers that all can benefit from, brainstorm together, and parcel through all of the elements as a group. It's easier to teach new material this way, but, as teachers, we know the realities. Not all students, especially if not accustomed to reading their work in front of others, will want to get up in front of an entire class, or even a small group, and read aloud (some middle school students would be devastated!). Because of this, it would be best to introduce them first to buddy sessions, at least for the read-aloud part—in short, begin with the whole class for introduction and/or review of the steps and protocols, then re-form students into buddy sessions. In the whole-class sessions, all students are responders, so writers have the benefit of many different feedback types, as do the responders in practicing feedback. In buddy sessions, students are more limited, albeit more private and intimate. Buddy pairs can always be brought back together for debriefing after writers and responders have worked through all the steps and protocols.

Much of the initial decision making will depend on how much time is available for language arts or English instruction, the size of the classroom, the comfort level of students when reading their work to peers, and, of course, your students' knowledge of and extent of practice with goal setting, identifying trouble spots in their writing, and communicating what type of feedback they want from their peers. The extent of prior practice will drive how much and what you must teach them before actually implementing the peer-coaching process (Chapters 5, 6, and 7 contain lesson plans to prepare students for each step). Following is a description and rationale for the exercising of each class model within the peer coaching process.

Whole Class

Using a whole-class model is recommended for initially rolling out the process by modeling and teaching the class the writer and responder steps and protocols. Begin with the model lessons for teaching Step One found at the end of Chapter 5, where students are introduced to the concepts of setting goals, identifying issues, making feedback choices, and preparing to listen. Lessons for Step Two, found at the end of Chapter 6, cover summarizing and active listening. These lessons are to be followed by the teaching of Step Three, which uses modeling strategies to teach the integration of feedback into the writing drafts. Lessons for teaching Step Three are found at the end of Chapter 7. When all steps have been introduced, students can be released to buddy sessions for practice in giving and receiving feedback, one as writer, the other as responder, interchangeably. After practicing with buddies, bring them back to whole class for debriefing. Continue in the next session with more focus lessons, releasing students again for practice in buddy or group sessions to read their drafts aloud for giving and receiving feedback. Once they have assimilated the process, students will simply move into groups or buddy sessions as needed (like magic!).

Groups (4–5 Students)

As in the whole-class model, teaching the initial process in groups is recommended after all students have been given minilessons on the various skills required for success: goal setting, establishing trouble spots, active listening, making feedback choices, and using and implementing the various forms found in Part III. In groups, all students are responders, while writers, after communicating their goals, issues, and feedback choices, individually share their writing drafts. When writers finish reading, they will call on one responder at a time to give feedback while taking notes or gathering notes taken by responders while listening. Forms for note taking are in Part III, and they are discussed in the Roles section that follows.

Buddies

As with group instruction, students must first be taught a succession of lessons to facilitate their peer-coaching efforts; these lessons familiarize them with required skills, such as goal setting and issue identifying. Buddies provide a more personal forum for students to exchange feedback and a safe haven of sorts for those reluctant to share their work with peers. I recommend that buddies be alternated so that students receive a variety of peer feedback from which to choose.

In all settings, daily or regular minilessons can address student weaknesses, which teachers are able to identify when circulating among students during peer-coaching sessions. Figure 1.1 outlines how each of the roles would operate within each class setting.

SCHEDULING FOR INSTRUCTION

At first glance, fitting the peer-coaching program into a regular school day can be tricky. However, I've discovered that with careful scheduling, difficulties can be easily surmounted. Figure 1.2 outlines a typical 60- to 90-minute literacy block implementing the process once students are trained in the steps, roles, and protocols. Both middle school block scheduling and high school English period scheduling can easily accommodate themselves to the program. The next chart, Figure 1.3, outlines peer-coaching implementation in a typical 30-minute language arts class period.

STUDENT ROLES AND THE FORMS TO HELP THEM

The remainder of this chapter includes a complete description of the student roles and the tasks within each role, as well as a delineation of all the relevant forms found in Part III as they apply to the functioning of each of the roles. These forms are tools for students to use when setting goals, when deciding what they need help with (issues), and when making feedback choices. Teacher forms, in

Figure 1.1 Managing Student Roles in Different Class Settings

Whole Class	Groups	Buddies
Writer and Responder	Writer and Responder	Writer and Responder
Teach the requisite skills at each step: goal setting, identifying issues, making feedback choices, summarizing, articulating feedback to the writer. Move students into buddy sessions for Steps Two and Three, or have one student at a time read her or his piece aloud to the class. When writers read to the entire class, each student becomes a responder.	Requisite skills are taught through minilessons before grouping (4 to 5 students per group). The writer communicates goals and issues to all responders. Responders provide feedback to the writer orally, with the writer calling on one at a time for feedback and writing down feedback notes as needed.	After practicing with the requisite skills in the whole-class setting, writers and responders are paired up for Steps Two and Three to give and receive feedback interchangeably. Ideally, students will switch buddies throughout the drafting stages, or the teacher can assign different buddies.
Whole Class	Groups	Buddies
Manager, Editor	Manager, Editor	Manager, Editor
Assign one manager and one editor for every three groups of students, or three managers and three editors for 30 students. Managers circulate when students are peer coaching to coach and monitor proper effort. Editors begin circulating *after* all students have received feedback, including the editor if necessary (often, editors are students who finish early). Once feedback has finished, editors will begin looking for clues or signals from students that need editorial assistance.	Assign one manager and one editor for each group of students (groups of 4 to 6). Managers will begin their work immediately; editors will circulate after all students have gone through the feedback process, working with students one-on-one using one of three editor's forms. Students will let the editor know when they are ready for editorial assistance or use an established system of clues, such as placing a pencil off to the side to indicate they are ready for assistance.	Assign three managers and three editors for every 15 students—or six for a class of 30 (when possible). The same procedures are used for managers and editors as in the whole-class and group sessions, with managers circulating and students signaling when they need or are ready for editorial assistance.

Figure 1.2 Peer-Coaching Literacy Block Model (60 to 90 Min.)

Minutes	Activity
15–20	Silent writing time (students continue working on drafts, begin new drafts, or prepare material for peer coaching).
10–20	Review and practice (when necessary) of a step or protocol within a step: goal setting, identifying issues in their writing, or active listening.
30–40	Peer coaching with buddies or in groups: asking for feedback, giving feedback, and receiving feedback.
10–20	Students return to their writing to make changes, import feedback, or work with editors.

Figure 1.3 Peer-Coaching Language Arts Class Model (30 Min.)

Day	Activity	Minutes
Day 1	• Silent writing (or writing silently) • Lesson or lesson review of skills (goal setting, issue identifying, active listening, etc.)	5–10 20–25
Day 2	• Peer coaching • Review/debriefing	20–25 5–10
Day 3	• Silent writing (or writing silently) • Lesson or lesson review of skills (goal setting, issue identifying, active listening, etc.)	5–10 20–25
Day 4	• Peer coaching • Review/debriefing	20–25 5–10
Day 5	• Silent writing (or writing silently) • Lesson or lesson review of skills (goal setting, issue identifying, active listening, etc.)	5–10 20–25

Note: Eventually, when students understand and have mastered the feedback process, sessions in both models move to writing and peer coaching recursively. Students peer coach as needed, with the teacher circulating among them, taking anecdotal notes, offering suggestions on feedback choices, and ensuring that students are using the protocols properly. Proper use of the protocols involves helping students formulate specific suggestions and coaching their feedback responses: "*When might we want to select the* I heard *choice?" "What situation would call for* No Feedback*?"* and so forth.

addition to the student forms, are also included in Part III (and are outlined in successive chapters as they become relevant). These reproducible student tools are listed and described below.

The Writer Role: Responsibilities and Related Forms

In addition to producing the initial draft, which is the subject of the peer-coaching process, writers must also read their drafts out loud to a peer buddy or to peers in a small group, unless extenuating circumstances dictate otherwise (speech impairment, loss of voice, modifications, teacher discretion). All students will function in this role at some point.

• As the content for the session, writers must bring a writing piece or draft prepared prior to the session. They may also create one at the outset of the peer-coaching session during silent writing time. Since goal setting takes place in the very early stages of development, the draft will guide the development of a goal. Students may, and often do, change their goals throughout the course of working over a draft.

• Step One: *Establish goals and issues, and make a feedback choice.* These are the forms that will help writers with Step One:

○ **Goals List (No. 1)**. This checklist will help students determine a goal using a think-through process. Writers will distinguish their goal distinct from the project's goal or the teacher-assigned goal.

o **Identifying an Issue Checklist (No. 3).** Using a think-through, this checklist will help students determine, from among possibilities, what they might want or need help with.

o **Feedback Type Checklist (No. 5).** This checklist offers five choices for feedback: (1) feedback on goals, (2) feedback on issues, (3) feedback on goals and issues, (4) "I heard . . ." feedback, or (5) no feedback. (See Chapter 5 for more detail.) If no feedback at all is wanted, and writers simply want to read, they may request the No Feedback option, but only once per draft. Students will still receive "I liked . . ." feedback with this option.

- Step Two: *Summarize and read.* Once the goals and any needs are communicated, the writer must summarize the writing piece briefly and then read it aloud to peers so that responders can come back with the feedback asked for. These are the forms that will help writers with Step Two:

o **Writer Summary Organizer (No. 14).** This form will help students pare their writing down to its most essential and important elements, so they can summarize the piece in a minute or less, according to the Step Two protocol.

o **Oral Reading Rubric (No. 15).** This rubric sets oral reading expectations for effective communication of student-writing drafts through verbal and nonverbal presentation techniques that include intonation, pitch, intended message, poise, eye contact, and persuasion.

- When writers finish reading in a whole-class or group setting, they must call on one person at a time to give them feedback. If they are in a one-on-one buddy session, the writer and responder will take turns—one reading, the other giving feedback, and then they will change roles.

- Step Three: *Decide what feedback to use.* Writers will take notes during and after the feedback session, reflecting on the important editorial decisions they are making. These are the forms that will help them with Step Three:

o **Writer Reflection Organizer (No. 12).** Writers fill out this form after the feedback session to reflect on feedback offered before deciding what to keep and what to leave out.

o **Self-Feedback Checklist (No. 8).** This form is used when students need to self-coach or work through the peer-coaching feedback process independently (the form is a tool for self-coaching), as well as when incorporating Step Three for making decisions. Writers are walked through a think-through process on feedback to reconcile their goals, issues, and feedback selection. Writers may also use this form to take notes on while receiving feedback from responders.

The Responder Role: Responsibilities and Related Forms

Responders must listen specifically for what writers establish as issues, as goals, and as a feedback type wanted. This is an important role, and all writing and drafting efforts hinge upon how effectively responders are able use active listening skills to develop productive feedback responses. Because responders have the serious responsibility of tailoring their feedback to exactly what was listened for, they need to listen intentionally, actively, and with purpose. In turn, they must respond with and articulate clearly not only what they heard but also what they liked and what writers asked for. Lessons that teach the listening protocols can be found in Part II, Chapters 6 and 7.

- Step One: *Listen for the goals and issues.* Responders will take notes as needed while writers read their drafts, and they listen with intention to what the writers' goals and issues are for the writing piece. With much to listen for, responders are always encouraged to ask questions of the writers before giving feedback. These are the forms that will help responders carry through on Step One:

  - **Active Listening Checklist (No. 6).** This checklist helps responders position themselves for listening actively and with purpose by focusing on body positioning, body language, mental referencing, referencing goals and issues, and other tips for listening purposefully and actively.
  - **Good Listening Rubric (No. 16).** This rubric makes student responders aware of the expectations for active listening while providing them with a tool for monitoring progress and rising to the expectations.
  - **Peer Feedback Checklist (No. 7).** To position their listening, responders note writers' goals, issues, and feedback selection. This checklist also prompts them to ask questions and provides a think-through list of prompts for later feedback consideration. While this form is useful in implementing Steps One and Two for listening, it is also useful as a reflective piece in Step Three.

- Step Two: *Listen to the piece as it is read (listening with a purpose).* Responders will take notes before writers read aloud and also during the reading, recording thoughts for later feedback. These are the forms that will help responders with Step Two:

  - **Peer Feedback Checklist (No. 7).** Responders record writer feedback while listing information in Sections 1, 2, and 3 for note taking and reflection.
  - **Responder Reflection Organizer (No. 13).** After listening, responders fill out this reflection sheet to reflect on thoughts and notes taken to position what they are going to give as feedback to writers.

- Step Three: *Give feedback to the writer.* Responders first say something positive using an "I liked . . ." statement before offering any other feedback suggestions, then they follow with "I heard . . ." statements, and continue with helpful, focused feedback without using the word *you.*

- In place of "you" statements, students will use "I" statements for offering suggestions, such as *"I might try . . . ," "I have tried . . . ," "I would . . . ," "I heard . . . ."* The word *you* can only be used within an "I liked" statement such as, *"I liked how you . . . ,"* or inside of a question such as *"Have you tried . . . ?"* The following forms, also used in Step Two, will help Responders in Step Three:

- o **Peer Feedback Checklist (No. 7).** Section 4 offers suggested prompts for beginning feedback statements, such as *"I liked the way . . . ,"* *"I might try . . . ,"* and *"Has this been tried . . . ?"*
- o **Responder Reflection Organizer (No. 13).** Responders refer to this form to reflect (again) on what they heard, what the goals and issues were, writers' feedback selection, and any thoughts that came to them while listening to position themselves for giving the writer feedback.

TEACHING TIPS FOR THE WRITER AND RESPONDER ROLES

- If students are apprehensive about reading their work in front of others, allow them to buddy up with a partner of their choice until they warm up to the process, especially if peer coaching in a whole-class or group setting. Allow them to reconvene with larger groups after they have read and received feedback.
- Certain instances may call for the writer role to be shared by two peers—one writing, setting the goal, the issue, and the feedback type, while the other reads the piece out loud. In such instances, appoint a reader, or have the student select one—someone he or she trusts or has an established working/peer relationship with. This technique might also be used as part of the protocol *initially* to ease writers into reading aloud.
- Practice listening protocols, such as those behaviors named on the **Active Listening Checklist (No. 6)** and the **Good Listening Rubric (No. 16)**. Practice across all content areas and in multiple situations—casual, formal, at home, or in any peer discussions related to class work. Encourage students to use journal reflection on their experiences.

Editor Role: Responsibilities and Related Forms

Though all writers should and will ultimately serve as editors for their own writing draft, a peer editor will help writers on several levels during the drafting process and throughout successive sessions. The editor's role is introduced only after students understand, are comfortable with, and have had plenty of practice with all three steps in the writer and responder roles. Editors circulate among students as assigned by the teacher, although a few may volunteer. (See Figure 1.2 for editor classroom grouping.) Editors begin their work *after* students have completed peer coaching in Steps Two and Three, the giving and receiving of feedback, and have resumed working on their drafts.

Editors can be helpful with struggling readers and writers or students identified as needing academic assistance in whole-class, group, or buddy sessions. Good student editors can offer more personal guidance focusing on areas relevant to the protocol—goal setting, issue identifying, feedback type, summarizing, feedback decision making, grammar, punctuation, and other

English usage. The following forms, found in Part III, will help editors carry out their responsibilities:

- **Editor's Before Coaching Checklist (No. 9).** Editors record writers' feedback choice, goals, and issues as identified while helping them through a think-through process designed to solidify and clarify the feedback.

- **Editor's After and Between Coaching Checklist (No. 10).** Editors offer assistance in successive rounds of student peer coaching, particularly as it applies to incorporating feedback. Editors work writers through another thinking process (1) to reconcile feedback with goals, issues, and the feedback choice, and (2) to help decide what feedback is most useful so that it can be incorporated into the writing piece.

- **Editor's Final Checklist and Rubric (No. 11).** Editors help writers with the final stages of their draft, particularly in incorporating feedback into the writing—solidifying goals, reconciling feedback with what was asked for and what will be most useful, and using feedback that helps with issues identified. The rubric portion of this checklist will help writers and editors check for grammar, proper syntax, and usage by focusing on ideas and content, word choice, and conventions.

The Manager Role: Responsibilities and Related Forms

The manager role is introduced once students have an understanding of the writer and responder roles, as well as the total process. It is by far the most popular role, particularly among my middle school students. Those who may struggle with conceptualizing the process, and especially struggling writers who are reluctant to write and share their work, often want to "play" the role as manager. Students who become managers have the opportunity to observe, orchestrate, and conceptualize while fulfilling a need to be successful. In high school, the manager position is a natural fit for those who finish their writing early, need a break from their writing, or demonstrate leadership tendencies. The role also tends to build students' confidence in the process as a whole, adding a comfort level to reading aloud in front of peers, setting goals, asking for help, and articulating feedback. The manager role also provides students with a sense of responsibility and ownership. Like the editors, managers will float among groups, buddy sessions, and whole-class sessions. Managers should

- Organize and keep track of the student peer-coaching session, including helping the teacher organize the classroom, hand out proper forms, and orient others to their groups or buddy sessions;

- Remind students about the steps and protocols within the steps, for example, using "I liked . . ." statements and avoiding the word *you;*

- Alert the editor to someone who may be ready for his or her assistance;

- Use the **Manager's Checklist (No. 17)** to check off the proper execution of role steps, protocols, and responsibilities for writers, responders, and editors.

TEACHING TIPS FOR THE EDITOR AND MANAGER ROLES

- Usually, students who finish their final draft early like to volunteer to be editor. Ideally, these are the students to assign to the role if the teacher is assigning them. They tend to be the more proficient writers, capable of, and good at, offering other writers individual editorial assistance.
- If editors, either assigned or volunteered, need to continue working on their drafts through a round of peer coaching, allow them to—their work does not begin until students have finished giving and receiving feedback. If they have no draft to work on, allow them to sit in as a responder before they begin to execute their responsibilities.
- Editors, when paired properly with writers, can be a wonderful resource to struggling writers. Consider floating editors that focus in on struggling writers.
- Develop a system that students can use to indicate they need the assistance of an editor when in buddy or group sessions, such as placing a card upside down on their desk or placing their pencil in a designated spot. Editors can pay attention to these cues for assistance and respond without having attention called to students' needs.
- Managers can be particularly helpful in strengthening those students who are apprehensive about the process or who are struggling to conceptualize it. Consider allowing students who are struggling to be managers, even though they may be behind in their work. Placing trust in them can go a long way in their transitioning as well as boosting their confidence in all parts of the process.

Student peer-coaching roles contribute immensely to the building of enthusiasm in the writing process. In addition to the steps and the protocols within the steps, taking on a role facilitates for both middle and high school students a strong sense of community, responsibility, and ownership in their writing and the writing of their peers. Peer coaching is team effort made stronger by the roles that students assume to work collaboratively toward a single goal: that of writing improvement for each and every class member.

2

Silent Peer Coaching and Peer Coaching as Questioning

> *The phrase "one question naturally leads to another" catches the spirit of the proposed solutions and serves as the criterion and guideline for sequencing topics . . . . Then the logic of inquiry is guiding the design.*
> —Wiggins and McTighe, *Understanding by Design*

In *Understanding by Design,* authors Wiggins and McTighe (1998) suggest that we teachers organize our lessons around tasks that have clearly delineated goals and objectives; that with thought-provoking, open-ended questions, we move students forward with priority and with purpose. Likewise, activities take on a greater purpose and deepening of cognition when students articulate what they need for their writing by establishing end goals, trouble spots, and feedback type, while working through intentionally to an end result. *Silent peer coaching* and *peer coaching as questioning* are student coaching options that may in fact be *better* options for *some* students, depending upon priority and purpose.

SILENT PEER COACHING

Silent peer coaching is student peer coaching that is carried out silently with writing instead of speaking. When properly used, this method can quickly transition to an internal process, offering students an opportunity to read what they may already have heard, thereby resulting in more focused, personal feedback. Silent peer coaching may also be a better option for students that are in somewhat isolated academic environments, such as home schooling, in-house detention, or small, pull-out classes. In addition, it's a comfortable option for students not yet ready or able to articulate verbally for any number of reasons.

Usually, I introduce students to silent peer coaching after we've practiced with and mastered regular student peer coaching in the writer and responder roles. Because communication is conducted through back-and-forth writing, silent peer coaching employs no oral reading or summarizing of writing pieces. Students make necessary changes by completing a self-directed feedback review process using the **Self-Feedback Checklist (No. 8)** for Steps Two and Three, and responders read the piece silently. Invariably, my student responders appreciate the approach because it allows them an opportunity to respond from another perspective—as reader versus listener.

THE WRITER ROLE IN SILENT PEER COACHING

The silent peer coaching process follows the same steps and protocols as traditional student peer coaching—goal setting, issue identifying, making feedback choices, and deciding what to keep and what to leave out. After responders review the writers' checklists to find out their goals, issues, and feedback choices, responders read the writing piece silently. (In the lesson plan that follows this description of the roles in silent peer coaching, you will also find the forms that writers will use to communicate this information to the responder.)

THE RESPONDER ROLE IN SILENT PEER COACHING

Once the goals, issues, and feedback choice are communicated to the responders via the written forms and the piece has been read silently by the responder, the responder will reflect on feedback using the same forms named below. Next, the responder will articulate feedback to the writer through writing and turning the forms over to her or him. (The forms to be used are listed in the lesson plan that follows.)

After reviewing the forms, the writer is ready to work on Step Three—editing the writing piece. If editors are being used, this is when they will step in. What follows is a template of a lesson plan outlining the flow of written interaction among peers in silent peer coaching. This lesson is used best in buddy sessions, but it may also be used in small groups.

Lesson Plan for Silent Peer Coaching—Buddy or Group Sessions

1. Hand out **Peer Feedback Checklists (No. 7)** to student responders to document the writer's goals, issues, and feedback choice. Instruct responders to complete the forms for the writer they'll be working with by reviewing the writer's following paperwork:
   - Goals List (No. 1, Step One)
   - Identifying an Issue Checklist (No. 3, Step One)
   - Feedback Type Checklist (No. 5, Step One)
   - Self-Feedback Checklist (No. 8, Steps Two and Three) from a previous session
   - Writer Reflection Organizer (No. 12, Step Three) from a previous session

2. Allow writers 5 to 10 minutes to complete their forms and another 5 to 10 minutes for students to exchange papers.

3. Remind responders to complete the following and have them ready for use when giving feedback:
   - Peer Feedback Checklist (No. 7, Steps One, Two, and Three)
   - Responder Reflection Organizer (No. 13, Step Three)

4. After responders complete a reading, allow them to take two to three minutes to complete the **Responder Reflection Organizer** and the **Peer Feedback Checklist** before handing the information over to the writer (remember, it is silent, so they will not be speaking the feedback; writers will read the feedback on the forms).

5. When necessary, remind peers of the responder protocols ("I liked . . ." and "I heard . . ." statements).

6. Encourage writers to take notes on the **Writer Reflection Organizer** after reviewing feedback from responders. Coach them through the process.

7. Integrate the editors, who assist writers in deciphering and deciding on what feedback to use and import into their writing piece. Remind editors to use the **Editor Checklists (Nos. 9, 10, and 11)**. Point out that where writers are in the drafting process (before, during, or post-peer coaching) determines which checklist is used.

   a. Circulate, coach, and take anecdotal notes as students pursue their roles as writers, readers, and editors.

   b. Encourage writers to question readers on feedback for clarity. Encourage writers to consult editors in interpreting and integrating feedback.

c. Allow writers time to use the **Self-Feedback Checklist (No. 8)** to determine what feedback to use while applying a self-coaching method to incorporate goals and issues with feedback received.

8. If time is available, lead a debriefing session on the process—how it went, what were the problems, what students liked best, and how they felt about the process. Ask them all to make an "I feel . . ." statement about how they liked or may not have liked silent peer coaching compared with regular student peer coaching.

TEACHING TIPS FOR SILENT PEER COACHING

- If the forms become too cumbersome for writers to use (there are five for writers and two for responders), instruct writers to use only the **Self-Feedback Checklist (No. 8)** because it houses information on all three steps.
- When working in groups, have writers copy their drafts before the session, so they are ready to disseminate them among the four or five readers in their group. At the end of the feedback session, when all responders have finished writing their feedback on the **Peer Feedback Checklist (No. 7)** and **Responder Reflection Organizer (No. 13)**, tell the writers to gather the feedback sheets to review while they complete their **Writer Reflection Organizers (No. 12)**.
- Introduce editors when all writers have had their drafts read through a round of peer coaching. Editors will continue to work silently, completing the applicable **Editor's Checklists (Nos. 9, 10, and 11)** to give to the writer.

PEER COACHING AS QUESTIONING

Peer coaching as questioning moves students from the mechanics of coaching and the process of writing to the higher-order thinking that moves information and end products forward, primarily through the use of questions. As in the basic peer-coaching model, writers set goals and issues before establishing a feedback type; this segment of the process is guided by the prompts on Part III forms specific to peer coaching as questioning, namely the following:

- **Goals List for Peer Coaching as Questioning (No. 2, Step One)**
- **Identifying an Issue for Peer Coaching as Questioning (No. 4, Step One)**
- **Feedback Type Checklist (No. 5, Step One)**
- **Self-Feedback Checklist (No. 8, Steps One, Two, and Three)**
- **Writer Reflection Organizer (No. 12, Step Three)**

In this modified peer-coaching approach, responders may also help writers through the goal- and issue-setting process using questions as outlined on the **Goals List** and **Identifying an Issue for Peer Coaching as Questioning.** Writers communicate goals, issues, and feedback type through questions— much as in the game *Jeopardy.* Responders provide follow-up feedback through more questioning; all feedback is provided in the form of a question, either a clarification-seeking question or a feedback question.

In advanced sessions, when students have used this approach two or more times, writers can respond *back* to the responder's feedback questions (see the transcript at the end of this chapter). Since questioning challenges and deepens thinking, a back-and-forth questioning approach between writers and responders can be productive.

This type of peer coaching is a challenging method that invokes thinking at higher, deeper, and more creative levels; it is recommended that it be taught and practiced repeatedly to master fully. This method is especially effective across multiple content areas, such as science, social studies, and math, where questioning works to present and clarify, deepen and broaden, investigate, solidify, and clarify key ideas (Wiggins & McTighe, 1998). (See Chapter 5 for examples of statements turned into questions for peer coaching as questioning.)

A Sample Transcript: Peer Coaching as Questioning in the Classroom

It might be helpful to see how this type of peer coaching can play out in actual classrooms. Students in grades six, seven, and eight participated in eight 90-minute literacy blocks of peer coaching. The following transcript is from Session 6, their first experience with peer coaching as questioning. The writer indicated that, to reach her goal, she needed help with her introduction. Her issue was that she typically struggled with introductions. I was particularly interested—and totally surprised—to observe how the writer responded to the questions.

Responder 1: Maybe she could put what city or town that they lived in . . .

Teacher: How could you make that a question?

Responder 1: Could you put the city or town that they lived in?

Writer: He's going to be in Pennsylvania, the person is.

Responder 2: Do you want to write a town in Pennsylvania?

Writer: I could do Philadelphia.

(silence)

Teacher: Anyone else have questions, and if you have trouble thinking of a question, tell me what the suggestion is, and I can help you turn it into a question.

Responder 1: Why is the mother making the pie?

Writer: She is making it for the celebration . . . Wait, couldn't she be making it for the celebration that she's going away from?

(Note how the writer responds back to the responder with a question, rather than answering her directly.)

Responder 2: Let me think . . . Why are they having a celebration? Wouldn't that be sad?

Writer: (undaunted) Could they be wanting it to be happy?

Responder 1:   Could it be like sad kind of, or could it be happy, or could there be feelings in there about him going away?

Writer: Could they be trying to be like making it so he is not sad? I think I should add more about them being sad. And maybe I could make it more interesting and have one of the sisters sneak into his nest.

(Note how the writer stops fielding questions back to the responder and begins to problem solve with affirmative statements.)

Responder 1:   Could they take his rifle?

Writer: Could they just come with him and want to go? Could they want to run away because they don't want to be at home and be bored?

Responder 1:   Could you ask about their excitement on September third?

Responder 2:   Could you write about him and his brother or something?

Writer: Yeah, that would be cool! He's going to bump into John.

TEACHING TIPS FOR PEER COACHING AS QUESTIONING

- Introduce peer coaching as questioning once students fully understand the student peer coaching process, in particular the roles of writer and responder. If introduced too soon, the process will be counterproductive, and students will not use it properly. When used properly, questioning works well to further higher-order thinking.
- With students, brainstorm questions for each area on the **Self-Feedback Checklist (No. 8)** form since it covers all three steps. This will help to acclimate students to the thinking behind questioning to reach solutions.
- Using the forms specific to peer coaching as questioning, extend the question prompts by brainstorming other questions geared to eliciting important information from the writer—information focused on goals, issues, and feedback types.
- I always begin these sessions by telling students that we'll be peer coaching, but we'll be doing it "like *Jeopardy!*" Watch out, because those who play *Jeopardy!* will catch on very fast!

Notice how the writer responded back with questions, and how those questions, coupled with those fielded by the responders, worked into some solutions for developing the piece. This is the essence of peer coaching as questioning.

Both silent peer coaching and peer coaching as questioning provide options for meeting a variety of student needs for multiple learning styles and differentiation of instruction. While neither approach may be the option of choice for all sessions or a specific session, these approaches may work into other areas depending upon the teaching goal, project goal, and student abilities. Use them as they apply to given tasks, while understanding and appreciating their unique contributions to deepening student thinking.

3

Scaffolding Responsibility to Adolescent Writers

> *Placing work a bit out of the reach of a learner and then ensuring that the learner extends his reach and succeeds at the new level is at the heart of high-quality teaching.*
>
> —Carol Ann Tomlinson, *Fulfilling the Promise of the Differentiated Classroom*

Scaffolds are the support mechanisms construction workers use to reach a target that wouldn't be reachable otherwise—like the roof on a three-story house or a skyscraper in New York City. In the learning process, scaffolds help student learners to do what they wouldn't otherwise be able to do on their own (Vacca & Vacca, 2005). Varying grouping and giving students access to tools and materials are some ways we can scaffold curriculum and instruction (Tomlinson, 2003). Scaffolds help learners acquire a new skill or strategy until it can be assimilated internally. So although scaffolding is about helping and hanging on, it is also about letting go.

I've found the most challenging part of scaffolding to be knowing *when* to let go and then *what* to do next. How do I know when students are ready to work independently in student peer-coaching sessions? What are the signals that they're ready, the signs that they understand the process? And then, how *much* can I let go of, or how much can the student let go of, at one time? It's really about trial and error—for us as teachers *and* for them as students. The best news is this: If we didn't call it right the first time, we can always step backward and reclaim a piece of that scaffold until we can let go again . . . and again and again if necessary. Students need to know this too—that if they need to reclaim the support of an organizer, a checklist, or a review of the steps on a poster, they can use it as much as they need to and try letting go again later. This is trial and error at its finest!

THE GRADUAL RELEASE OF RESPONSIBILITY

Remember, peer coaching isn't so much about teaching teenagers *how* to do it as it is to gradually release their reliance on the tools they use to integrate the process—organizers, checklists, rubrics, and our coaching. Only teachers can decide what setting will best facilitate a scaffolding of responsibility when introducing students to peer coaching. This chapter will establish some guidelines to use when making these decisions.

The rule of thumb I use as a gauge for overall readiness is to give students an entire course of peer coaching for one writing piece after they've been taught all the steps and protocols within the steps (goal setting, issue identifying, summarizing, etc.). Fully training students in all of the steps and protocols takes anywhere from four to six lessons, depending upon how much experience they've had with those skills. So, after they've been trained and through a set of peer coaching activities focused on one draft (about two to three rounds), try assigning them a writing task with either less support or no support. For example, when goal setting would require using the **Goals List (No. 1)** to help students think through the project's goals, instruct them to write their goal at the top of their paper prior to writing, or early in the draft. Where they would use the **Identifying an Issue Checklist (No. 3)** to establish trouble spots, tell them to write beneath their goals, at the top of their draft, whatever it is they'll want help with. When they've become accustomed to this revised method, move on to the next phase of letting them go. Tell them to think of their goal for a moment and what they want help with, and then to immediately articulate it to the responder. By doing this, teachers are handing over responsibility to students in manageable chunks.

If at any juncture where adolescent writers are struggling—for instance, if they can't seem to remember their goal—take them back a step, and have them begin writing it on their drafts again; if they begin to struggle with thinking of a goal, return them to the **Goals List** to employ the think-through, again allowing them to access whatever process they've internalized as it mirrors the process in the tools they've used. Figure 3.1 outlines guidelines for scaffolding, including when and how to let go.

Teachers should introduce the editor and manager roles to their students as the growing peer coaches demonstrate readiness to handle them, introducing the roles either in follow-up to whole-class session, in group sessions after a practice first-draft whole-class session, or as floaters within buddy sessions. All of this, of course, comes after teachers have modeled each piece of the process for the students (each lesson in Chapters 5 through 7 includes modeling components).

It is with a similar mindset, and in the same manner, that we must *take* away some of the supports for thinking, such as the various checklists, without taking away any accountability for the thinking they support, weaning the students from the checklists and organizers, allowing them the leeway they need to internalize the process. It is a fine balancing act.

Ideally—if taught daily in 60- to 90-minute literacy blocks—within six weeks, students will be conducting peer-coaching sessions on their own as buddies or in groups or as needed while you circulate around the room taking anecdotal notes, offering individual assistance, evaluating, and making observations. Some may be working independently with peer coaches as needed, while others may remain in groups with more guidance and use of forms as they transition to more independence. Your letting go will actually enable the students to hold on longer, stronger, and tighter to what they know is effective practice. To judge the range and extent of their progress over time will require attention and flexibility. This is why the **Teacher Anecdotal Notes Records (Nos. 18–21)** found in Part III will be important: These forms offer good information to move forward with when planning instruction.

GUIDELINES FOR SCAFFOLDING

Figure 3.1 offers specific guidelines for deciding when and how to scaffold for independence, when and how to let go, and what behaviors and performance

(Text continues on page 26)

Figure 3.1   Guidelines for Releasing Responsibility to Writers and Responders

Form and Step	Performance Indicators: When to Let Go	Transition to Independence: How to Let Go
WRITER		
STEP ONE **Goals List (No. 1)** Writers establish direction for their writing, either before beginning it or in the very early stages, by virtue of the goals they set. Goals tend to be recursive and are not necessarily static throughout a draft (students can change goals as they continue drafting).	• The writer can immediately respond with writing goals without referring back to the project's goals, and/or • The writer can immediately respond with writing goals in Section 4 on the Goals List without completing Sections 2 or 3. Note: This behavior indicates a consciousness of goals when making decisions about what is needed in feedback.	• Have writers fill out "Genre and assignment type," then go directly to No. 3 to indicate their goals. • If the writer is able to go directly to a goal in successive sessions on other drafts, skip this form altogether, allowing students to write goals on top of their drafts. • When goals are immediate and students can remember them, have students immediately articulate the goals to peers without writing them on their drafts.
STEP ONE **Identifying an Issue Checklist (No. 3)** Writers decide what they need help with on a specific draft. This will often be what they typically struggle with but may change from draft to draft.	• The writer is able to articulate with clarity where the trouble spots or issues are without using Section 1 or 1a on the checklist. • The writer immediately goes to Section 3 on the checklist and can finish at least one prompt quickly and with clarity. • The writer knows after the first round of peer coaching where the challenges or struggles (issues) are in the writing piece.	• At first, have student writers go directly to Section 3 on the checklist and complete at least two of the prompts. • After a round of peer coaching, allow students to write their issues on top of their drafts, beneath the goals. • Once students are quick at identifying trouble spots, allow them to immediately articulate them to the responders without writing them down. • If students struggle with remembering issues, return to writing them down. If they struggle to establish them, return them to the checklist.
STEP ONE **Feedback Type Checklist (No. 5)** Writers decide on a feedback choice to focus the responder's listening attention to what the writer wants in feedback.	• The writer is capable of working quickly through the checklist or bypassing some sections while making appropriate feedback selections that align with issues, identified goals, and the writer's strengths. • The writer makes appropriate feedback choices without using the checklist. • Feedback received is productive for the writer, who is able to use	• Allow writers to go directly to the Goals List to document their feedback choice (rather than work through the Feedback Type Checklist) while articulating their feedback choice directly to the responder. • Instead of using the checklist, allow writers to review the feedback choices from the poster, make a choice, and then write it down on top of their paper.

(Continued)

Figure 3.1 (Continued)

Form and Step	Performance Indicators: When to Let Go	Transition to Independence: How to Let Go
	it in the drafting process (indicating that feedback choices are appropriate and align with the writer's goals and areas in need of help).	• After writing down their feedback choice several times on their drafts, have writers articulate their feedback choice directly to responders without use of the checklist or writing it on their paper. Note: Allow writers to return to the checklist as needed (needs may vary depending on genre, content, etc.).
STEP TWO **Writer Summary Organizer (No. 14)** Writers readily highlight the most salient aspects of their piece to articulate prior to reading aloud.	• The writer does not need to work through every question on the organizer before writing out a full and accurate summary; or • The writer moves directly into writing the summary after answering two or three questions; or • Once the main idea questions on Nos. 4 through 7 (at minimum) can be bypassed before going directly into writing the summary at the end of the form. • The writer does not need the summary at all and can quickly articulate the major themes of his or her work in a minute or less.	• Writers can be directed to write out the summary without the organizer after reminding them that it must include all major events and take no longer than one minute to read aloud. • Once written out, have them rehearse their summaries with the editor or another peer for cross-checking against the organizer. • As student writers transition into writing summaries without the organizer, no rehearsal or cross-checking will be necessary—allow them to articulate the summary directly to the responder. Note: Encourage their return to the organizer as needed in other content areas or with different writing projects.
STEPS TWO and THREE **Self-Feedback Checklist (No. 8)** After a review of their draft, writers will automatically apply a think-through process to know what needs to be changed and how to change it.	• The writer moves directly to Nos. 5 or 6 on the checklist without working through Nos. 1 through 4, knowing precisely what his or her piece needs improvement on and what will be applied as a result of having reviewed it both aloud and silently. • Writers will know what feedback to apply without using the checklist, and they will immediately begin to apply it to their drafts.	• Allow writers to immediately write down thoughts for revision directly onto their drafts, during and after the feedback sessions, without use of the checklist. • Encourage their review of any former feedback to complete this process, independent of using the checklist. Note: Allow them to return to the checklist as needed.

Form and Step	Performance Indicators: When to Let Go	Transition to Independence: How to Let Go
STEP THREE **Writer Reflection Organizer (No. 12)** Writers readily reflect on goals, issues, and feedback in writing, and they then immediately return to their drafts to make editorial changes.	• The writer immediately transfers and remembers feedback from the responder onto the Reflection Organizer. • Students bypass No. 4 on the Reflection Organizer and immediately begin applying feedback onto their drafts.	• Transition students from using the Reflection Organizer, and allow them to go immediately to their drafts and begin incorporating feedback and making desired changes.
RESPONDER		
STEPS ONE, TWO, and THREE **Peer Feedback Checklist (No. 7)** Responders listen actively and intentionally to reconcile feedback with protocols, writing goals, and feedback requests.	• The responder goes directly to Section 5 of the checklist without the reminders and think-through of Sections 1 through 4. • Upon quick reflection, or in conjunction with the Responder Reflection Organizer (No. 13), the responder can expeditiously think of and articulate appropriate feedback to the writer focused on what she or he asked for in feedback. • The responder is able to remember the writer's goals, issues, and feedback choice before immediately articulating appropriate feedback to the writer.	• Allow student responders to respond to the writer immediately without using the think-through process of the checklist. Note: Allow them to return to the checklist as needed (the need may vary according to genre, content, or how effectively the responder articulates feedback to the writer).
STEPS TWO and THREE **Active Listening Checklist (No. 6)** Students listen actively and with purpose by exhibiting certain behaviors, assuming postures, and taking notes as reminded by the checklist.	• The responder reviews feedback requests and/or seeks clarification prior to the writer's reading aloud, positioning himself or herself for active listening. • The responder no longer needs to be reminded of the checklist items, such as keeping writer information handy, where to find it, body positioning, note taking, and so forth. • By all appearances, and based on effective, focused feedback to the writer, the responder is exhibiting good listening behaviors. • The responder is scoring in the 15 to 24 range of the Good Listening Rubric (No. 16).	• Review, or point student responders to, the Active Listening Checklist poster (No. 36) in place of their working through the checklist. • With or without the poster review (let them know it is always there should they need it), allow them to begin listening immediately. • Continue to have students rate each other, or themselves, on the Good Listening Rubric (No. 16) to determine if they need review in this area or a return to using the checklist.

(Continued)

Figure 3.1 (Continued)

Form and Step	Performance Indicators: When to Let Go	Transition to Independence: How to Let Go
STEP THREE **Responder Reflection Organizer (No. 13)** Responders reflect on listening to articulate appropriate feedback to the writer.	• The responder takes notes while listening, noting immediate thoughts and afterthoughts. • The responder is able to readily articulate appropriate and applicable feedback, after the writer reads aloud, with little review or need to complete No. 4 on the organizer.	• Responders bypass Nos. 1 through 3 on the Responder Reflection Organizer if they can respond immediately with appropriate "I liked . . ." and "I heard . . ." statements. • Responders bypass the reflection organizer and immediately give feedback statements to the writer.

indicators to look for. Weaning the blossoming writers gradually and appropriately from constant use of checklists, organizers, and other thinking aids will continue to move them closer to that internal dialogue. They can return to them when needed, but remember, the ultimate goal is that they assimilate the thinking behind the thinking aids as an internal process.

TEACHING TIPS FOR THE SCAFFOLDING OF RESPONSIBILITY

Here are some tips for carrying this scaffolding process out.

• Allow students opportunities to try out their own method or tweak the materials as they need to, re-creating forms and checklists using less of the think-through or making them more consistent with a specific project or content area. This will help them take ownership of the process on an individual level as well as allow them to internalize it in a language that might better lend itself to long-term storage and retrieval.

• In addition to transitioning them to writing goals and issues on the top of their drafts (versus using the checklists), alternate this with students' using blank paper to write down their thinking process as it mirrors, or aligns with, the organizer, checklist, or rubric. For example, when they are completing Step One, have them write down their goals on blank paper or in a journal, calling it their Feedback List. This can be followed by a statement of their issues and their chosen feedback types. They can return to the Feedback List in another session, especially if some time has elapsed since they've had a session. This will transition them to the internal process, and eventually they won't need to write all of their goals down—instead, they'll think them through.

• Observe how rapidly writers select their goals, identify a feedback type, and roll in feedback from peers. The quicker they apply this thinking process, the more obvious it will be that they've assimilated the peer coaching process, and the less likely it will be that they need the more formal support materials.

Behavior and performance when student peer coaching are the tell-all indicators for knowing when to allow for the "next steps" in the transition process that moves students closer to independent application of the peer coaching process. It is important that students understand the protocols as *catalysts* to the acquisition of important skill sets, communication, and a code of conduct that will result in success and application across all content areas. The delegation of responsibilities to students should be gradual, with responsibilities doled out in age-appropriate increments, and contingent upon the mastering of manageable student peer-coaching skill sets—goal setting, issue setting, active listening, identifying trouble spots, problem solving, and effective editing. Student ownership and internalization will occur naturally and concurrently with a gradual release of responsibility from teacher to student, then student to self. These are strategies that will help transition adolescents not only academically but also to and through the passages of their ever-unfolding (and often complicated) lives.

4

Facilitating and Assessing the Program

> *Putting a grade on top of a paper often erases the student's own evaluation of the work. As teachers, we should not be the only voice when it comes to assessing the quality of a piece of writing. We want students to evaluate their work as well.*
>
> —Fletcher and Portalupi, *Writing Workshop: The Essential Guide*

Remember, the ultimate goal for our students is writing autonomy and the development of an internal process for revision that is applicable to any writing circumstance. What does this mean? That, eventually, we can take off the teaching hat and breathe a sigh of relief, letting students work through the sessions doing what they need to do, while we circulate to monitor, supervise, offer individual assistance (coach), take anecdotal notes, and gather formative assessment data. This is good management. But first, you will need to be the coach that trains the coaches—sort of like turnkey training for the classroom! It all begins with teacher modeling.

TEACHER MODELING

As teachers, demonstrating our own self-coaching process when teaching the student peer-coaching model helps students acquire a level of comfort within it, transitioning them to the more guided instruction that will follow. Identifying our own needs within our writing pieces, setting our own goals, providing our own effective feedback, and deciding on what feedback we can use are all practices we can model for our middle and high school students. Demonstrating a feedback exchange, for example, with a fellow teacher or with a student can make the difference in students' transition from theory to practice. It is always a good idea, particularly if the protocols are new concepts for them, to model the process in its entirety before setting your students off on their own.

Suggestions for Teacher Modeling

Remember, reading their work aloud may be a huge risk for some students, especially if they're feeling insecure about themselves as writers or are particularly guarded about their inner selves, as many students are. With this in mind, creating a secure environment for student peer coaching and the teaching of writing is absolutely essential. When classrooms are perceived as safe, students will take the mental, emotional, and intellectual risks that result in cognition and creativity (Jensen, 2005; Kirby, Kirby, & Liner, 2004; Tomlinson, 2003; Wolfe, 2001). Not only will those students who exhibit insecurities flourish under a secure classroom environment, but students will also benefit from it. Modeling the process can help create that safe, nurturing environment, a crucial component in students taking that first step. What follows is a transcript of teacher dialogues that provide specific examples of language teachers can use when modeling the various aspects of student peer coaching.

Steps One and Two

Teacher 1 as Writer:	I wrote this piece back about two years ago, on a summer vacation my husband and I took in Spain. We climbed

Mt. Gau, and I wanted to write about the awesome experience. My goal was to have the reader feel what I felt when I reached the summit of the mountain. I also thought I'd send it out for publication or enter it into a contest.

(Teacher reads it aloud.)

Step Three

Teacher 2 as Responder: I liked the personal touch given in the essay through very vivid and detailed descriptions of the mountainside, the village you walked through to get there, and how you felt as a stranger in Spain. I felt as if I were there, but I might feel more there if there was a little more talking about it—unless there wasn't any speaking, which I would understand because it sounds so awesome!

(Teacher 1 laughs and responds that there was, in fact, much talking. Notice the absence of the *you* word as a suggestion in Teacher 2's response.)

Teacher 2: So, then, maybe write up some of that dialogue. I'd like to hear it as it was actually spoken to make it seem even more real. I think that publishers like to publish this sort of realistic view of something this awesome, and it would stand a better shot at getting published.

(Note again, that the teacher, with the exception of the "I liked . . ." phrase, did not use *you*; rather, Teacher 2 kept it objective using *it* or *I might*, demonstrating options to using *you* for students.)

Step Three

Teacher 1: Let's see . . . What were my goals for this piece? (Teacher 1 looks back at the **Goals List, No. 1**.) Ah-hah—that's right; I wanted to make the reader understand how I felt when I reached the top, and I wanted to enter it into a contest or get it published— so, it needs to be really good, really polished, as good as it can be. Do I think it is that, or better yet would I send it out as it is now? Not quite yet . . . So, what else do I need to do? Well, maybe I'm getting ahead of myself . . . Let me go back to my first goal of making the writer feel like I felt, or understand how I felt, at the top. One of the suggestions was that I write up some of the talking between my husband and me on the way up; it might make the reader feel it stronger or understand it better. Also, how did I feel . . . (Teacher 1 jots down some notes in the margin, brainstorming how she felt while climbing.) So, I think I'll include some of this when I rewrite, have it peer coached again, and then think about polishing it up to send out.

Note how this teacher thought through all of the feedback given and then reconciled it with her original goal set by cross-checking with the **Goals List**.

Reconciling feedback with goals and needs established at the onset is the purpose and intent of the forms.

Shown through the above dialogue, it is important that, when modeling, teachers think through the entire task: Don't hold back. Let students hear how we struggle with the protocols, first perhaps in swaying toward the tendency or habit to say "you" but then correcting ourselves.

PROGRAM ASSESSMENT
ALLOWING THE INFORMAL TO DRIVE THE FORMAL

We know that assessment-driven instruction, when effectively and responsibly carried out, results in improved student performance. The data derived from district or state standardized assessments are formal and contain statistical measures that support specific grade-level performance indicators. These are the assessments and indicators that are supported by the informal data that would result from student peer-coaching efforts. These efforts can be documented and then quantified through rubrics and other evaluation tools found in Part III. All of the evaluation tools contained in these sections are informal and performance based. When students master the art of each role within this process—writing, identifying needs, goal setting, problem solving, making critical decisions, listening effectively, and communicating feedback—they are rising to the expectations needed to be successful in independent assessment circumstances that require similar patterns of thinking, particularly those that require writing on demand.

We also know that assessment data must *drive* instruction, whether it is formal or informal, to be fully productive and useful. Given this, we need to regard student peer coaching as the "doing" part of what needs to happen. Observing students while in the doing will supply us with the insight needed to move forward in our planning, advancing them in their academic growth.

TEACHER EVALUATION AND OBSERVATION

Taking anecdotal notes will help to generate valuable observational and behavioral data. (**Teacher Role Evaluation Rubrics, Nos. 26–29**, found in Part III, will aid in this effort.)

Evaluating both the process and student role fulfillment, then gathering the results of this to evaluate them as end products, gives us a complete picture of adolescent writers as overall learners and performers within a deductive process. Their thinking, as demonstrated through writing, judging, problem solving, speaking, adhering to protocol, listening, and overall coaching, will present itself clearly. Use of this informal data will aid us in moving them closer to adopting permanent, internal solutions that work to inform them in related independent-learning efforts.

Once groups are organized and students have acclimated themselves to the peer-coaching process, teachers will be freed up to circulate among group or buddy sessions, taking anecdotal notes that home in on team performance, peer collaboration, proper execution of steps and use of protocols, and overall individual progress within the process of successful role execution. The **Teacher Role Evaluation Rubrics**, while more formal, offer a numeric score through use of an evaluation slide at the end of each rubric. These rubrics will aid teachers in making the kinds of decisions needed to develop next steps in planning for successive coaching sessions, follow-up lessons, and reporting to district or state administration and parents. More important than the overall rubric score, however, will be its usefulness in informing teachers of individual student progress on the skills within the respective roles.

PEER EVALUATION

In addition to rubrics and checklists, students will have other opportunities to evaluate and coach each other as they execute their roles and responsibilities using the Peer Evaluation Rubrics. Because peer role evaluation is student-to-student and part of the coaching process, there are no evaluation slides. Students will discuss and encourage one another in their efforts as they monitor and evaluate performance based on specific protocol indicators. Teachers can make independent decisions on the use of this information (student-teacher conferences, parent conferences, facilitating peer conferences, portfolios, student folders, etc.). Figure 4.1 lists the skills to be assessed in each role

Figure 4.1   Skills for Each Role, and Forms to Help Assess Them

Role	Skills	Relevant Forms
Writer	Editing, prewriting, peer review, revising, writing style, problem solving, speaking, communicating, verbal articulation, oral reading, critical analysis, reflection, summarization, and identifying main idea	• Teacher Anecdotal Notes Record for Writers (No. 18) • Teacher Role Evaluation Rubric for Writer (No. 26) • Peer Role Evaluation Rubric for Writer (No. 22) • Oral Reading Rubric (No. 15, Step Two)
Responder	Active listening, speaking, communication, editing, peer review, note taking, problem solving, critical analysis, reflection, summarization, and collaboration and teamwork	• Teacher Anecdotal Notes Record for Responders (No. 19) • Teacher Role Evaluation Rubric for Responder (No. 27) • Peer Role Evaluation Rubric for Responder (No. 23) • Good Listening Rubric (No. 16, Steps One and Two)
Editor	Editing and revision, prewriting, peer review, problem solving, communication, critical analysis, reflection, identifying main idea, and collaboration and teamwork	• Teacher Anecdotal Notes Record for Editors (No. 20) • Teacher Role Evaluation Rubric for Editor (No. 28) • Peer Role Evaluation Rubric for Editor (No. 24)
Manager	Problem solving, coaching, leadership, communication, evaluation, collaboration, leadership, organization, reflection, teambuilding	• Teacher Anecdotal Notes Record for Managers (No. 21) • Teacher Role Evaluation Rubric for Manager (No. 29) • Peer Role Evaluation Rubric for Manager (No. 25)

and the related reproducible resources in Part III that can be used by the teacher or a student peer to evaluate those skills.

The informal evaluation effort that is part of peer coaching will help students continue to take responsibility for their progress as writers, and for all the steps, skills, subskills, and any other "baby steps" needed along the way. All of this will result in a successful writing effort that works itself into polished writing pieces. Ultimately, students will perform better on all assessments, including the formal, high-stakes assessments used in their respective states. In this sense, the informal drives the formal.

TEACHING TIPS FOR PEER EVALUATION

- Rotate student evaluators within groups so that all have an opportunity to observe and to be observed. Students can rotate as an evaluator in turn, evaluating one at a time. For example, the evaluator evaluates one student as both writer and responder, along with any other role taken; or the evaluator evaluates each student in the group as writer and responder. Editors will be evaluated by writers, and managers evaluated as assigned.
- Since all students are responders, have the entire group or class evaluate the writer. When finished, the writer can gather the evaluation forms and read them, drawing his or her own conclusions about progress, tweaking himself or herself accordingly.
- The editor can only be evaluated by the writer since only the writer will know the degree to which the editor was helpful. Be sure that writer and editor have the opportunity to pair up and evaluate each other.

PART II

The Model in Action

In Part II, the three chapters address the three steps of the peer-coaching process in greater detail, as they unfold in the classroom. Chapters 5, 6, and 7 provide instruction, examples, transcripts, and model lessons for implementation. Below is the matrix you saw in Part I, now divided into the applicable steps and ensuing protocols covered within each chapter.

CHAPTER 5

ROLE: Writer	ROLE: Responder
Step One:	*Step One:*
Establish goals and issues, and make a feedback choice.	***Listen for the goals and issues.***

• Communicate your goal for the writing.
 • Decide what issues you need help with.
 • Select a type of feedback:
    1. Feedback on goals only
    2. Feedback on issues only
    3. Feedback on goals *and* issues
    4. "I heard . . ." feedback only
    5. No feedback (only available once)
	• Listen carefully for what the writer says his or her *goal* is for the writing piece (take notes, ask questions).
	 • Listen carefully for what the writer says she or he *needs* help with in feedback, or the issues. Ask clarifying questions when necessary.

CHAPTER 6

Step Two:	Step Two:
Summarize and read.	***Listen to the piece as it is read (listening with a purpose).***
• Summarize your writing in one minute or less. • Read your piece aloud to the responder.	• Listen to provide feedback. • Employ active listening.

CHAPTER 7

Step Three: *Decide what feedback to use.* • Take what you need (in feedback), and leave out what you do not. • Make adjustments to your writing.	*Step Three:* *Give feedback to the writer.* • First, say what you liked best using "I liked . . ." followed by "I heard . . ." statements. • Next, offer feedback focused on what the writer asked for. • *Do not* use the word *you* in a statement unless it is a question or in an "I liked . . ." phrase.

Step One

Establishing Goals and Issues

> *Goal-setting conferences allow for one-on-one exchanges that are difficult to come by in busy classrooms. They also foster students' understanding and ownership of their own learning.*
>
> —Carol Ann Tomlinson, *Fulfilling the Promise of the Differentiated Classroom*

As you will recall from Part I, the first step of the peer-coaching process requires the writer to establish the goals for the piece, establish an issue or trouble spot, and then decide on a feedback type. All this gets communicated to the responder or responders, who in turn listen actively and respond with helpful feedback.

STEP ONE FOR THE WRITER
ESTABLISH GOALS AND ISSUES, AND MAKE A FEEDBACK CHOICE

- Communicate your goals for the writing.
- Decide what issues you need help with.
- Select a type of feedback:
  - Feedback on goals only
  - Feedback on issues only
  - Feedback on goals and issues
  - "I heard . . ." feedback only
  - No feedback (only available once)

In the transcript that follows, it is clear that goal setting was new practice to this eighth-grade student, as is peer coaching. When students set goals for their writing, they establish purposes for moving forward in their remaining writing efforts, thus resulting in the polishing and completion of their finished products.

Student Transcript—Goals, Issues, Feedback Choice

Writer: I want it to be published, and I hope people like it. People will buy the book if it will be published. I want this piece to get readers' attention. I want people to see what happened to people in medieval times. Get it published.

Teacher: Tell us what kind of feedback you want.

Writer: I want suggestions for the beginning, because in the beginning I didn't really have an opening sentence. That's pretty much it.

Teacher: What kind of feedback?

Writer: Goals and "I heard . . ." feedback.

Teacher: You'll always get "I heard . . ." feedback, so you can just ask for goals.

Writer: Goals. I want feedback on getting this so it will be published.

As demonstrated above, Step One involves several decisions; to complete that step, writers must establish and articulate what is needed to move forward in the writing effort. To take this giant three-tiered step, student writers must

- Set a goal; a goal statement may sound like this:

  I wanted it to make the reader think. I also wanted it to be more like an idea, more like a dream than something real. I also always wanted it to be in Neil Gaiman's clear style. (Mina Elwell, Grade 7)

- Establish an issue or trouble spot; an issue may be expressed like this:

  I want to know if the beginning has enough information. I want to know if it explains enough about the characters. If the dialogue is clear, if the events are clear. (Russell Ng, Grade 8)

- Select a feedback type from among the five feedback choices; a feedback type choice may sound like these:

  I want feedback on my issue (used when the writer really needs help with something).

  I want feedback on everything (meaning feedback on goals and issues).

  I want "I heard . . ." feedback only (a popular choice).

Students don't usually ask for feedback on their goals only, but it remains an option they can and at times do exercise. The most popular feedback requests, from my experience, continue to be the "I heard . . ." feedback and feedback on issues only.

Let's break it down.

Writer Establishes and Articulates the Goals

Communicate Your Goals for the Writing

The rationale for goal setting is simple: When young writers understand where they need to end up in a project, they'll have a much easier time figuring out what they need to do to get there. Stating a goal is pretty straightforward and can begin with a statement as simple as "*My goal for this piece is . . .*" Yet, middle school and even high school writers may not be experienced at setting goals for their writing. The first time students go through this process, it is my experience that goal statements run the gamut—from finishing a writing piece, to adding more adjectives, to simply getting started. Goals usually focus on what students are struggling with, but they can also tie in to the project or assignment goals as set by the teacher or the writing project. As illustrated below, the writer's goals should not only be personal but also flow out of the project's goals.

> It is much easier to stay focused if you have your goals in mind.
> (Wade Carmichael, Grade 12)

Project/Assignment Goals ⟶ Writer Goals

Write a dramatic story.

Readers will understand what it's like to have a disability.

To clarify this relationship, Figure 5.1 illustrates how project goals serve as the impetus to developing personal goals for a piece of writing designed by the student in response to the project goal.

Figure 5.1   Examples of Project and Personal Goals

Project Goal	My Goal
Learn about a famous composer by writing a biography.	• To learn about Ludwig van Beethoven's life and what it was like for him to be a boy. • To be able to find my information on the Internet in less than three days. • To write a long piece with lots of detail. • To finish it.
Learn about the history of a local landmark.	• To find out the history of my house; maybe it was haunted! • To locate the right information in a short period of time. • Make it sound interesting to someone else, so they feel like they live there.

The first appendix at the end of this chapter, Lesson 5A, provides a concrete plan for teaching goal setting. In this lesson, students are prompted to complete a **Goals List (No. 1),** which includes consideration of the project goals.

In addition to teaching Lesson 5A, explore with the class some examples of goals statements prior to teaching the goal-setting activity. Establish possible prompts with your students and then place them up on a chart for reinforcement and future referencing (I keep these samples up for as long as several weeks—students appreciate them). Below is a session transcript that shows an actual goal-setting activity.

Student Transcript—Goal Setting

Writer (Grade 7):	I have a new goal. I want to change it and make it be awesome.
Teacher:	So, that's what you want help with too?
Writer:	I did my first one, and I changed it a lot.
Responder (Grade 8):	What do you want help with?
Writer:	I think . . . to make it awesome.
Teacher:	What will it take, what will your next step be, to make it awesome?
Writer:	More detail.
Teacher:	What was your first goal?
Writer:	To change it. So now it can be to give it more detail.
Teacher:	Go ahead and read.

(Writer reads.)

Teacher:	(to Responder) If you don't know her goal, you need to ask her to clarify, so you can listen for it. Do you have your Peer Feedback Checklist handy? Also, your Reflection Organizers, so you can write any thoughts down right away?

Commentary: In addition to demonstrating a writer setting and articulating a goal that changes within the course of one draft and several peer-coaching sessions, the above dialogue illustrates students moving from general goals to more specific goals.

Writer Establishes and Articulates Needs

The following student transcript demonstrates how the goals the student writer identifies will lead to the issues to be addressed by the responder.

Responder (Grade 7):	What is your goal?
Writer (Grade 6):	If I can make people know what it is like and feel how a disabled person feels when they wake up in the morning and can't walk.
Responder:	OK. Good goal. So what is your issue?
Writer:	I need to give it enough detail so readers will know what it is like to have a disability like that.
Responder:	Good. So summarize it a little bit, and then start reading.

From the goals flow the issues:

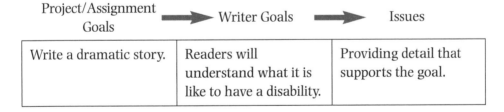

Project/Assignment Goals	Writer Goals	Issues
Write a dramatic story.	Readers will understand what it is like to have a disability.	Providing detail that supports the goal.

Writers' issues are anything students are struggling with in the present writing piece, what they have typically struggled with in the past, or expect to struggle with in the near future while working on their drafts. Identifying and then stating such issues (what struggle is anticipated), however, may not be a simple matter. For those teenage writers reluctant to share their writing in the first place, having to admit a problem with their writing is risky behavior! To allow reluctant students a comfort zone to work within when reading their writing aloud for perhaps the first time, students can elect, once per writing piece, feedback type No. 5, the "No Feedback" option. However, writers still need to articulate their issues and be open to receiving feedback in successive sessions. Lesson 5B, the second appendix at the end of this chapter, outlines a 15- to 20-minute lesson for teaching students the various feedback choices available for their use.

What if writers don't have an issue, or what if they simply don't know yet what they're struggling with? They always have the "I heard . . ." feedback option, encouraging peer coaches to respond using "I heard . . ." statements, in essence, moving from a focus on particular areas of struggle to a more general, all-inclusive response.

Responders orient themselves to focus on the goals the writer sets, so with or without any issue identified, there is always plenty available to coach with. The **Identifying an Issue Checklist (No. 3)** found in Part III provides students with a think-through for aiding them in the issue-identifying process.

Writer Establishes and Articulates a Feedback Type

After writers establish goals and issues, they need to select the type of feedback to be received *before* beginning the reading aloud portion. Students may select from five feedback choices:

1. Feedback on goals only

2. Feedback on issues only

3. Feedback on goals and issues

4. "I heard . . ." feedback only

5. No feedback (only available once per draft)

Figure 5.2 offers examples of feedback statements taken from actual student peer-coaching sessions.

Figure 5.2 Examples of Feedback Statements

Feedback on Goals	Feedback on Goals and Issues	"I heard . . ." Feedback Only
I heard the process used to name the fish. (Goal was to name the fish.)	I liked the detail that made it longer and more interesting. (Goal was to add more detail; issues were in making it longer and more interesting.)	I heard how Stanley's mom made him write and how Stanley did not want to. I might try to make it sound more like his mom has the problem, not him! (Issue was to create conflict with the characters; the project's goal was to create a problem-solution in writing.)
I heard a title that made me want to hear more. (Goal was to think of a good title.)	I liked the way it begins by telling about the boy and where he's from. It's like, he doesn't want to really go there though—does he want to be in the Olympics? I heard a young boy who could someday be in the Olympics, but it might be good to include excitement about it. (The project's goal was to write about a	I heard him tell everyone not to race him. I heard how he felt about it. (Student wanted feedback on goal; goal was to make the readers understand how the character feels.) Have you tried using a thesaurus to get some more descriptive words? Sometimes when I use more description and detail, it makes

Feedback on Goals	Feedback on Goals and Issues	"I heard . . ." Feedback Only
	"trophy you'd like to win." The issue was that he was too young to join the Olympics and consequently did not know where to begin.) *When I don't know how to start something, I ask my dad what it would be like.*	*my writing easier to understand.* (This responder used the word *you* but quickly reclaimed responsibility by giving an example of his own resolution to a similar issue.)
I heard something that could get published. (Goal was to "be published.")	*There might be room for some more action in the beginning after the motorcycle part . . . Ummm . . . maybe rides and stuff, and description.* (The goal was to include action and description; the issue involved a struggle with providing detail.)	*I heard a lot of action in the beginning, and lots of vrooms from the motorcycle, but then it sort of dies down. I would like to hear more action and other stuff other than motorcycles because lots of noise means action.*

TEACHING TIPS FOR STEP ONE (WRITER)

- Using a matrix as an organizing tool, work with students in cultivating their own goals by aligning them with the project's goals. To develop the matrix, place the project's goals on one side and the students' stated goals on the other.
- Encourage students to keep a record of goals either in their journals or on their drafts to revisit at later points when they might need an idea.
- Feedback can change from one student peer-coaching session to another—allow students this flexibility and encourage it. As students need to adjust their goals and change their issues, they'll also need to change the type of feedback they receive. How wonderful that they will be able to make these choices rather than instructors making the choices for them!
- Be sure to review the steps and procedures as a class before students read with buddies or the class. Do this before beginning each step in the process until your adolescent writers can carry out the process without coaching. Keep the steps posters visible in the classroom for viewing as needed.

STEP ONE FOR THE RESPONDER
LISTEN CAREFULLY FOR THE GOALS AND ISSUES

- Listen carefully for what the writer says his or her *goal* is for the writing piece (take notes, ask questions).
- Listen carefully for what the writer says she or he *needs* (help with) in feedback, or the issue. Ask clarifying questions when necessary.

Students can always use repeated instruction and practice in listening, particularly when it comes to active listening. As responders, students will listen with intention through a mindset established by knowing what writers' goals and issues are, asking questions for clarification when necessary and appropriate, and taking notes. Two resources found in Part III, **Peer Feedback Checklist (No. 7)** and the **Responder Reflection Organizer (No. 13)**, should be used by the responders to guide themselves through these actions.

The first responsibility of responders is to report back to writers what they heard, leveraging this report with writers' identified goals and issues. A heavy load of responsibility, this task requires that responders be present, intentional, and proactive. Having been made aware of what the goals and issues are, responders develop an interest, or investment, in the process, making listening points more meaningful and deeper. These three specific tasks—taking notes while listening, asking questions, and reflecting on points after listening—all work together to complete the active listening process while facilitating the flow of meaningful, productive feedback to the writer. Lessons for teaching the protocols (Model Lesson 5C, Step One for the Responder: Active Listening for Goals and Issues, and Model 6C, Step Two for the Responder: Active Listening for the Feedback Selection) can be found at the end of Chapters 5 and 6 respectively.

TEACHING TIPS FOR STEP ONE (RESPONDER)

- Demonstrate the listening process using a metacognitive approach, thinking aloud; this approach is a powerful modeling tool for teaching these protocols.
- Facilitate active-listening sessions for practice. Have one partner speak to the other for about three minutes. Instruct the listeners to remember as much as they can about what was said. Assign a topic, something personal, like "Everything about yourself you can say in three minutes" or "Everything about your favorite movie or book in three minutes." Repeat this process several times, and by the third or fourth try, students will develop their own strategies. Debrief with a discussion of the process and strategies developed.
- Discuss and explore with students methods for taking quick notes—turning longer phrases into shorter ones—as they work within the protocols. For example, if a student thinks, "I like the way each character is introduced," shorten to "**character introduction." Stars or plus signs can delineate the positive; negative signs can indicate areas for suggestion. Or "I heard a lot of activity but did not hear a lot of dialogue" can shorten to "**activity. No dialogue." Students will be able to listen more effectively if they do not become too bogged down with the note-taking process.

To assist teachers in locating resource forms easily, Figure 5.3 below delineates the Step One forms needed for each of the peer coaching roles.

Figure 5.3 Forms for Executing Step One

Writer	*Responder*
• Goals List (No. 1) • Identifying an Issue Checklist (No. 3) • Feedback Type Checklist (No. 5)	• Active Listening Checklist (No. 6) • Peer Feedback Checklist (No. 7) • Good Listening Rubric (No. 16)
Editor	*Manager*
• Editor's Before Coaching Checklist (No. 9) • Editor's After and Between Coaching Checklist (No. 10) • Editor's Final Checklist and Rubric (No. 11)	• Manager's Checklist (No. 17)

APPENDIXES TO CHAPTER 5

Step One for the Writer

Model Lesson 5A: Establishing Goals and Determining Issues in the Writing Piece

Model Lesson 5B: Deciding on Feedback Type

Model Lesson 5C: Active Listening for Goals and Issues

MODEL LESSON 5A

Step One for the Writer: Establishing Goals and Determining Issues in the Writing Piece

Note: This lesson may also be used to prepare students for silent peer-coaching sessions.

Step: Step One—Establish goals and issues, and make a feedback choice.

Role: Writer

Content Area: All

Skills: Goal setting, problem solving, critical analysis, prewriting, brainstorming

Protocols:

Set your goal or goals for the writing piece.

Decide what you need help with, if anything.

Lesson Time: 30 to 40 minutes

Materials Needed:

- **Goals List (No. 1)**
- **Steps and Guidelines for Writer (No. 31)** poster
- **Identifying an Issue Checklist (No. 3)**
- Assigned writing project or something in the beginning stages of the student's choice
- Chart paper or whiteboard
- Projection device

Lesson/Student Objectives:

- Students will be primed for and prepared to execute their roles as writer in the student peer-coaching process.

- Students will know the difference between vague or overly general goals and actionable goals.

- Students will be able to set specific, actionable goals for the piece they are writing and establish issues (what they want help with) within their piece.

- Students will understand that project goals and personal writing goals tie together in the drafting process.

- Students will understand the distinction between a goal and an issue (a goal is where they want to end up; an issue is what they need help with).

Lesson Summary: Students will be queried as to their knowledge of and experience with the two protocols of Step One: setting writing goals and establishing their needs for help to achieve those goals. After a brief discussion of the difference between a goal and an issue, the teacher will use a personal experience to demonstrate and explain how goals aid in project completion and how identification of writing issues helps to make them better writers. Next, the teacher will brainstorm project goals and typical student goals with students. Before committing to a goal, students will be walked through sections in the **Goals List (No. 1)**. Before choosing an issue, students will also be familiarized with the **Identifying an Issue Checklist (No. 3)**.

Steps for Administration:

1. Ask students if they have ever set a goal before finishing a task or job. When hands go up, ask them what that task was (they might say to win a game or to finish a job at home, or they might give a project goal in another content area).

2. Ask students if setting the goal helped them. Then, ask what might have happened if they did not set goals—might they not have finished, or might the outcome have been different?

3. Explain to students that when you have a project to complete, you set a goal in order to get it done, explaining why goals are important (they give you something to work toward and help you finish what you started).

4. Give an example of something you did that required a goal (writing a letter to the editor at election time, winning a race or a contest). Or use your goal for them as students for your example. *My goal for you as students is for every one of you to love writing by the time the school year ends!*

5. Project out loud what might have happened if the goal you set was either different or not set at all—how it might have affected the outcome.

6. Position the **Goals List** for the entire class to view while working your own goal down the list, thinking aloud as you do.

7. Complete Section 1 on the **Identifying an Issue Checklist** while projecting it for the class to view, thinking aloud while working through it.

- *Hmmm . . . I haven't thought of any characters' names yet, I've just numbered them, so maybe I can ask for some help here.*

- *It's also historical, so I have to stick to the facts, and I am not sure if it sounds realistic, if all my facts are right. Might be nice to get some help here.*
- *So, I think I'll ask for . . .*

8. Brainstorm with students various goals for writing projects:
   - Winning a contest and getting money
   - Persuading opinions
   - Getting an A
   - Getting published and being famous
   - Making someone proud
   - Making how-to instructions understandable or workable
   - Writing a letter or resume to get a certain job
   - Completing something from beginning to end
   - Including detail
   - Leaving out unnecessary detail
   - Staying on topic

9. Ask students to think about a specific piece of writing they still need to finish, or use an assigned project for purposes of this lesson.

10. Place or position the **Goals List** for the entire class to view. Articulate the project's purpose or your goal for them in Item 1, Project Goals, if using an assignment specific for this lesson; then have them fill in Item 1.

11. Walk students through Items 2 and 3 on the **Goals List** *while you complete yours at the same time* for their viewing.

12. Discuss Items 2 and 3 on the **Goals List**, calling on students in turn to share their responses.

13. Have students complete Item 4, committing their goals to paper. Give students two minutes to discuss with, or recite their goals to, a partner.

14. Place the **Identifying an Issue Checklist** up for viewing by the entire class. Students should have their own to begin working on when ready.

15. Work through Sections 1 and 2 on the **Identifying an Issue Checklist** to identify and talk aloud about the details connected to the issue—for example, how the issue relates to the goal, how issues came about, what you usually struggle with, what you might do but aren't sure of yet (possible solutions). Let students *hear* your thinking process.

   a. If students are ready to begin working on their checklists, let them work as you continue to think aloud.
   b. Answer any questions that come up from students.

16. Have students explain to their coaching partner details about their issue (how they want help, why they feel they need help in this area, what they have already tried, etc.).

Intervention Modifications for Goal Setting:

Some students may continue to struggle with establishing a goal or completing one of the goal statements even after brainstorming, having it modeled, and hearing how others have responded to prompts on the **Goals List**. When this is the case, do the following:

1. Be sure they are clear about Project Goals on the **Goals List**. This will help them solidify their own goals if they are unsure.

2. Have students break their goals down into steps. Ask them

    a. What needs to get done next in this writing piece to make it to the project's identified goal? (It might be starting the writing, completing the writing, or adding another paragraph.)

    b. Have them write down the steps they need to take to achieve the goals. Write them down on chart paper for their referencing later.

    c. Continue to "chunk" these goals until they can become larger, such as "adding in adjectives," "giving characters voice," and so on.

Second-Language Modifications for Goal Setting:

1. In addition to reviewing the project goals with students, ask them questions to incite a dialogue about the project's ultimate ending place:

    a. What have you done so far?

    b. What will the next step be to get to the teacher's or project's goal?

    c. What will the next step be after that?

    d. What is your plan for this writing? What do you plan to write about?

2. If discussion doesn't result in any obvious goals, record students' answers and then repeat them back to them.

Examples:

Teacher: What have you done so far?

Student: I wrote the title, and I have the book I am going to use for the information.

Teacher: The project's goal is to have you write about a famous person. So what will your next step be now that you have your title and your source?

Student: Read and find the information to use.

Teacher: Here are two goals: One, read the book, and two, write down information to use in the essay. Bingo!

Intervention Modifications for Identifying an Issue:

Some students will say they do not have any issue in their writing, or they will struggle to find one. When this is the case, do the following:

1. Have students grade their paper as it is, using a class rubric or a subjective letter grade. If it is anything less than an A or satisfactory rating on the rubric, ask them to explain why, looking at areas that scored low. Often, an issue will emerge here.

2. Have students create a matrix or Venn diagram with "Project Goals" on one side and "My Goals" on the other side. In the middle, they will write out something that will help them get to their goal. Figure 5.4 compares project goals with personal goals and issues.

Figure 5.4   Project Goals, Issues, and Personal Goals

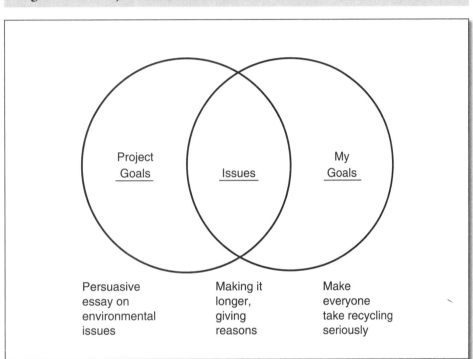

Second-Language Modifications for Identifying an Issue:

Have students draw out a continuum, with the project's goals on the right end, their own goals to the left, and the issues (blank) in the middle. See Figure 5.5 for an example.

Figure 5.5   Example Continuum

My Goal	Issue	Project Goal
Write an introduction.	Thinking of a trend. Knowing what a trend is.	Write an essay on global warming trends.

Often, when struggling students see what is expected in the end (the project's goal), then compare it to their own goal, they'll see where it breaks down and what they need help with. In this case, the student realized that without knowing what a trend is, the essay couldn't begin. Therefore, a struggle with the introduction was identified. The continuum provides a visual path by which students can problem solve their way to identification of an issue.

1. In addition to or replacement of the continuum, identify some key issues or goals using vocabulary words and terms, such as *describing,* or *developing character,* or *using voice.* Select words and terms students typically struggle to understand or that may be unfamiliar to them, and use those.

2. Place the terms on a matrix, and brainstorm substitute words and phrases that are understandable to them to clarify meaning.

    a. Example: For *using voice,* write, "sounding like me."

    b. Example: For *developing character,* write, "making people come to life."

3. Discuss all the words and phrases in the context of meeting the objectives for this lesson.

4. Revisit the issues or potential issues for their drafts with a new understanding of relevant vocabulary and terms as they apply to what they struggle with along with their writing goals.

Silent Peer Coaching: When using the silent peer-coaching method, students will write back- and- forth to a buddy or someone in the student peer-coaching group, helping with the details about his or her issue, further refining it, and offering suggestions to one another. When appropriate and possible, students may also use laptops or other instant communication devices to communicate back and forth on subjects within the **Goals List** and **Feedback Type Checklist (No. 5)**. This activity encourages their use of coaching language while allowing them time to discuss and uncover goals and writing issues using an interactive method they are accustomed to.

MODEL LESSON 5B

Step One for the Writer: Deciding on Feedback Type

Note: This lesson may also be used to prepare for silent peer-coaching sessions and includes steps for peer coaching as questioning.

Step: Step One—Establish goals and issues, and make a feedback choice.

Role: Writer

Content Area: All

Skills: Speaking, communicating, verbal articulation, problem solving, analysis, brainstorming, question generation

Protocol: Select a type of feedback:

1. Feedback on goals only

2. Feedback on issues only

3. Feedback on goals and issues

4. "I heard . . ." feedback only

5. No feedback (only available once)

Lesson Time: 15 to 20 minutes

Materials Needed:

- **Feedback Type Checklist (No. 5)**
- **Feedback Choices for Writer (No. 33)** poster
- **Peer Feedback Checklist (No. 7)**
- Chart paper or whiteboard
- Projection device
- Assigned writing project or a writing piece in the beginning stages

Lesson/Student Objectives:

- Students will be primed for and prepared to execute their roles as writers by deciding on a feedback type.
- Students will be able to identify a feedback type that works with their goals and identified issues for their writing piece.
- Students will be able to effectively articulate a feedback type to the class, the group, or their coaching partner.
- (For peer coaching as questioning) Responders will be able to articulate questions to coach the writers in reaching a decision about feedback.

Lesson Summary: Students will apply a think-through process for determining which feedback type is most appropriate for this stage of drafting. After a review of each feedback option, they will brainstorm ideas that might be relevant to each one. Students will then be led through the Peer Feedback Checklist, which is a think-through for the writers to help them decide what feedback option applies to their writing draft. The teacher will demonstrate this think-through process by thinking out loud while completing his or her own decision-making process and projecting it for viewing by all (writing directly on the overhead sheet or document imager). When students have completed their checklists, the teacher will revisit the original brainstorming session and make adjustments as needed, clarifying examples for each feedback type.

Steps for Administration:

1. Review the feedback options with students using the **Feedback Choices Poster for Writer (No. 33)** poster.

2. Brainstorm ideas for each option. Keep a list of these ideas placed where it will remain visible—on chart paper, whiteboard, or the overhead.

3. Place a copy of the **Peer Feedback Checklist (No. 7)** up for viewing by all. Check that students have individual copies in front of them.

4. Initiate a think-through process as you complete the checklist, writing in your own checks and comments while thinking out loud.

5. Think of one scenario for each feedback choice. Example:

I haven't really figured out what my goal is yet, and it's the first time I've ever read this aloud. I'm a bit nervous about reading aloud too . . . (check a couple of the areas) I've never received feedback on this either, so I think I'll exercise feedback option No. 5, but just this once because it is only available once per draft.

6. Allow students to work on their own checklists as you continue to think out loud.

7. Instruct students to complete it and decide on a feedback choice.

8. When all have finished, have students speak to their partners or their responders about their choices, comparing and contrasting them.

9. For silent peer coaching, have students exchange papers, read, and comment on them in writing.

Intervention Modifications:

1. Students may not know which choice to make, or may not make the most relevant feedback choice. They might have a glaring issue, for example, yet choose "I heard . . ." feedback or feedback focused only on their goals. If this happens, walk the student through each choice, posing additional questions to help the student decide which choice is most appropriate, at times creating questions for him or her to consider. Examples:

Writer:	I am not sure if I can meet my own goal.
Teacher:	What will you need to do to get to your goal? Is your issue related to your goal? (Suggest that she or he ask for feedback on goals and issues if they are related.)
Teacher:	Which is most important right now, your goal or your issue? (Suggest he or she ask for feedback on the one most pressing or important.)
Writer:	I have only written one paragraph so far (or may have written less). There isn't enough to give feedback on.
Teacher:	How far do you still have to go? Might that be your issue, or part of it? (Suggest "I heard . . ." feedback if the goal and/or issue still isn't clear.)

Teacher: (When a student seemingly made the wrong feedback choice, as in the example above) Are you sure about that? Think about what your issue is, or what you usually struggle with in your writing. Do you want some help?

If this process is new to them, students will often hesitate to receive feedback. In this case, remind them that the fifth feedback option, No Feedback, is only available once, and they will still receive "I liked . . ." feedback.

2. Have students who are still undecided or challenged by this assignment consult with three other students to check out their choice. Students who made a choice should explain how and why they made the choice.

   a. Instruct the students having difficulty to take notes while they are consulting the others.

   b. After all students have each checked in with three other students, instruct them to review the **Feedback Type Checklist (No. 5)** once more before finalizing their decisions.

Second-Language Modifications (Same as Above):

1. In addition to No. 2 under Intervention Modifications, pair each student up with another peer to take the notes so that concentration can focus exclusively on the responses.

2. Allow peers a few minutes to review the notes and discuss responses.

Peer Coaching as Questioning—Steps for Administration:

1. After completing the Steps for Administration, explain to students that the peer coaching as questioning method is similar to *Jeopardy!* (students who watch or play *Jeopardy* will immediately understand), where questions replace feedback responses.

   a. Query students briefly about their knowledge of *Jeopardy!*—how it is played, and how questions are developed. Students who play *Jeopardy!* will be very good at this method!

   b. Instruct students to work with a peer who will serve as responder to coach them on the think-through portion, making questions out of prompts on the **Feedback Type Checklist**.

2. Instruct students to work with partners on the think-through portion of the **Feedback Type Checklist** to develop their feedback type.

MODEL LESSON 5C

Step One for the Responder: Active Listening for Goals and Issues

Note: With modifications indicated (see Item 5 in Steps for Administration), this lesson may also be used to prepare students for silent peer-coaching sessions.

Steps:

> Step One—Listen to the piece as it is read (reading with a purpose).

> Step Two—Give feedback to the writer.

Role: Responder

Content Area: Writing in all content areas

Skills: Effective listening, verbal articulation, problem solving, critical analysis, reflection, interpreting author's message

Protocols:

> **Step One:** *Listen carefully for what the writer says his or her goal is for the writing piece (take notes, ask questions).*

> **Step Two:** *Listen carefully for what the writer says she or he needs help with in feedback, or the issues. Ask clarifying questions when necessary.*

Lesson Time: 50 to 60 minutes

Materials/Forms Needed:

Note: The first seven items are in Part III.

- **Role Descriptor Cards for Responder (No. 30)**
- **Steps and Guidelines for Responder (No. 32)** poster
- **Peer Feedback Checklist (No. 7)**
- **Responder Reflection Organizer (No. 13)**
- **Active Listening Checklist (No. 6)**
- **Good Listening Rubric (No. 16)**
- **Active Listening Checklist (No. 36)** poster
- **Goals List (No. 1)**
- **Feedback Type Checklist (No. 5)**
- Student writing draft

Lesson/Student Objectives:

- Students will be primed for and prepared to effectively execute their roles as responders in the student peer-coaching process.
- Students will apply active listening strategies by recording notes on the **Peer Feedback Checklist (No. 7)** to record the writer's goals, issues, and feedback choice.
- Student responders will listen effectively for the writer's goals as reflected in the writing piece.
- Student responders will respond with helpful feedback focused on what the writer indicated she or he needed help with (the issue).
- Students will respond using the type of feedback the writer asked for.

Lesson Summary: After the teacher engages the class in a goal articulation and feedback session based on the teacher's goals for the students, a discussion will ensue about the role of the responder as an active listener. The discussion will prepare students for understanding how to listen for the goals, issues, and feedback choices the writers establish in their feedback requests. By responding on the **Responder Reflection Organizer (No. 13)** first and then the **Peer Feedback Checklist**, students and student buddies will practice articulating goals, establishing issues, and overall listening to clarify and articulate feedback. Some students may need to practice for several rounds before feedback is clarified; ideally, teachers will be able to provide this opportunity. Finally, students will rate each other's progress using the **Good Listening Rubric (No. 16)**.

Steps for Administration:

1. Place the **Active Listening Checklist (No. 6)** for viewing by all, and review the list one line at a time.

2. Next, begin with 10 to 20 minutes of silent writing unless students have a prepared writing piece to use.

3. Remind students about the steps within both roles—writer and responder.
   - Ask them to recite the steps.
   - Review them together, using the wall posters.
   - Remind them that the posters are there to be referred to when needed.
   - Hand out the writer and responder role cards—have them read them over and discuss them with a partner.

4. Review and discuss the active-listening behaviors on the **Active Listening Checklist (No. 36)** poster

5. For silent peer coaching, have students apply active reading by taking notes and using the forms while they read, just as they would when listening.

6. After reviewing the responder's role card and responder steps on the poster, tell students that you would like their help with something. Begin with something simple such as how the last lesson went for them or how they like student peer-coaching sessions so far.

7. Tell them what your goal was for them (to become peer coaches, and be able to write and use the process without the teacher having to correct every single paper, having them become successful independent writers), offering a summation of what has been done so far.

8. Have students record this information on the **Peer Feedback Checklist** (sections 1 and 2).

9. Next, ask students for a feedback type, such as "I heard . . ." with feedback on the goal, and ask them how you've done as their teacher in reaching your goal so far. Ask them to first say something they liked using an "I liked . . ." statement.

10. Have students record this information on the **Peer Feedback Checklist** (section 4) before responding.

11. Encourage questioning (as per section 3 on the **Peer Feedback Checklist**).

12. Explain to students that this is how listening and responding works: the writer sets a goal, the responder listens to the writing piece to see if the goal is being met and gives feedback. Instruct students to read their piece aloud to a partner for buddy coaching—one is writer, the other is responder.

13. When silent peer coaching, have students read the piece silently, then write down feedback for the writer.

   a. Remind students to state the goals, issues, and feedback type to the responder before beginning to read. When silent peer coaching, have them write their chosen feedback type down for the responder, or let the responder read the writer's **Goals List (No. 1)** and the **Feedback Type Checklist (No. 5)**.

   b. Remind the students that writers communicate goals and issues to partners by referring them to their writer's **Goals Lists**.

   c. Remind the students that responders record the writer's goals, issues, and feedback type on the **Peer Feedback Checklist**.

14. Responders take notes on the **Peer Feedback Checklist** while the writer reads. When all writers have finished reading, bring attention to a projected copy of the **Responder Reflection Organizer**; responders in silent peer coaching will use the same form.

15. Prompt students through each section.

   a. Some students may have been filling it out while a writer was reading, in which case you should instruct them to finish it.

   b. Prompt them:

     • Think about what you liked the most, and write it down.

     • Next, think about what you heard in the writing, and write that down in the next box. For example, did you hear details, did you hear vocabulary that helped you visualize a picture, did you hear an author's unique voice . . . Think about the feedback your partner asked for.

16. Review each area on the **Responder Reflection Organizer**, checking off and reviewing one at a time.

17. Instruct all responders to review their **Responder Reflection Organizers** once more before filling out the **Peer Feedback Checklist**, Items 3 to 5, to confirm their responses.

18. Students team up once more to convey "I liked . . ." statements, "I heard . . ." statements, and any suggestions for feedback. When silent peer coaching, students write their "I liked . . ." and "I heard . . ." statements back and forth.

19. Instruct writers to use their **Writer Reflection Organizers (No. 12)** to reflect on the feedback after it is given.

20. Hold a class debriefing discussion on the process: Talk about what was easy, what may have been confusing, how the forms worked out, and whether the feedback was helpful. Answer any questions students may have.

21. Review the **Active Listening Checklist** poster once more, and have them complete a **Good Listening Rubric** for themselves.

Intervention Modifications:

1. Some students may need to have the writing read a second and even a third time to fully grasp the goals and issues and to respond with feedback focused on what the writer asked for. When this is the case, allow them to continue working with their partners, reading their pieces again, listening, and refining their responses on both the reflection sheet and checklist as needed.

2. Circulate and offer assistance in targeting and positioning feedback responses to make them productive. Students need reminders on the protocols and in referring back to information taken before and during listening on the **Peer Feedback Checklists**.

Second-Language Modifications:

Allow students to read, listen, and refine their responses on the forms as many times as needed for them to be able to articulate responses with understanding and clarity. Continue to coach them in this effort. Place another student in charge of this coaching effort when possible, allowing him or her to act as a manager for students in need of additional support.

6

Step Two

Summarizing, Reading, and Listening

> *I find that children and other adults are often better at seeing the one thing the piece is about than I am.*
>
> —Graves, *A Fresh Look at Writing*

After writers establish and communicate their goals, issues, and feedback choices, they'll then proceed to summarize their piece briefly—in one minute or less—and then read it aloud to their partner. At this juncture, responders bear the height of their listening responsibilities as they listen actively for the writer's goals (Were they met? Does the piece reflect his or her goals? How can it work closer toward them?) and issues (What can be suggested to help the writer with what he or she is struggling with?). Responders must also listen to position for offering the type of feedback the writer requested—feedback focused on goals, issues, or goals *and* issues, only "I heard . . ." feedback, or no feedback with "I liked . . ." statements. A tall order indeed!

STEP TWO FOR THE WRITER
SUMMARIZE AND READ

- *Summarize your writing in one minute or less.*
- *Read your piece aloud to the responder.*

The interchange below was one of the first group sessions after the formal teaching of the steps and protocols in a seventh-grade classroom. As the facilitator, I am still handing over responsibility to these students. While the activity involves both Steps Two and Three—summarizing, reading, listening, *and* responding, the focus is largely on the writer's summary, showing how students, when listening actively, are able to provide the writer with effective, focused feedback. Note how I interject to coach the student throughout the summary portion when she fails to deliver anything concrete. I also model an "I" statement as well as coach students at various junctures.

Student Transcript—Feedback Session

Teacher:	What do you want after it is read, in feedback? (Writer shrugs.)
Teacher:	Do you want to know what people think, some thoughts?
Writer:	Sure.
Teacher:	Tell us a little about it before you read it.
Writer:	It's a letter to a power company. (Writer indicates that she doesn't want to read it.)
Another student:	Would you like me to read it?
Writer:	Sure. (Another student reads the letter.)
Responder 1:	Wow. What made you want to write it?
Writer:	I think they should go green.

(Writer reads.)

Responder 2:	I like what you're doing, and I agree.
Responder 3:	I don't mean to be rude, but I don't believe in some of what you're saying because solar energy costs more, because the cells used for solar energy are expensive.
Responder 1:	It's true, but if more people built solar houses the prices would come down.
Responder 3:	You should try and state one main thing they should try to change, instead of burning fossil fuels.
Teacher:	Remember the protocol—using the word *you.*
Responder 3:	Oops.
Teacher:	How can you rephrase it? Remember the phrases (points students to chart paper with "I might . . ." and other "I" phrases written on it).
Responder 3:	I . . . I . . . I would try to say one thing to change.
Teacher:	You can also ask a question.
Responder 3:	(Thinks for a moment.) Does it have to be fossil fuels? (A discussion ensues about global warming and what students know about it—ozone, troposphere, alternative energy, ultraviolet rays, etc.)

(silence)

> Hold up! Doesn't she have to summarize it first?
>
> (Oji, Grade 7)

The Step Two process can be easily discerned from a careful reading of the above transcript. Briefly, after writers articulate their feedback choice, they summarize their writing piece in one minute or less prior to reading it aloud. Why place a time limit on the summary? Because writers will end up telling you every detail in the writing, completely bypassing the need to read it! It's also good summary practice—short, concise, pared down to its bare essentials—with some practice in paraphrasing and articulating the main idea. Lesson 6A: Summarizing the Writing Piece, at the end of this chapter, teaches summarizing for those students not accustomed to summarizing their own work. The **Writer Summary Organizer (No. 14)** in Part III will also aid the writer in development of this skill.

While the first part of Step Two requires students to pare their writing down to its essential elements and then communicate it in a minute or less, reading their piece aloud has its own protocols; for instance, they also learn about speaking in public and injecting voice into their writing. Tools to help them read aloud effectively are available in Part III through the **Oral Reading Rubric (No. 15)**. This step may take practice, and for a time, some students might be reluctant to participate. It is therefore recommended that teachers remain flexible in allowing students to have others read for them and in providing read-aloud practice in class, group, or buddy sessions.

A Second Student Transcript for Step Two

Below is a brief transcript of a writer and responder exchange between a sixth and seventh grader. The writer begins to read her piece immediately, before summarizing, as many students do. We teachers need to remind them until they get used to it—or as in this case, *they* remind each other!

Responder: So you want "I heard . . ." feedback?

Writer: (Nods. Begins to read the story aloud.)

Responder: Hold up! Doesn't she have to summarize it first?

(Teacher nods, directs students to the steps poster.)

Writer: It's a letter to a power company about going green. (Student continues to summarize.)

Responder: Are you writing to tell them how to go green?

Writer: No, I think they should go green. They probably know how, but I think they should. (Student reads aloud.)

STEP TWO FOR THE RESPONDER
Listen to the Piece as It Is Read (Listening With a Purpose)

1. Feedback on goals only

2. Feedback on issues only

3. Feedback on goals and issues

4. "I heard . . ." feedback only

5. No feedback (only available once)

Students know the drill for peer review: exchange papers, tell what you like, give feedback, make suggestions. It's the work in between that they need training on: how to respond to the writers' stated needs—that is, *to listen and respond actively.* Responders must tune in to the writer's goals for the piece so that feedback can be targeted, strategic, and focused; they must reconcile their feedback with the project's goal and with the identified issues. This step feeds directly into Step Three, teaching students to communicate this feedback precisely, meaningfully, and productively, so writers can make informed decisions, using this feedback to inform their next steps. Success with Step Three can only result from good listening, and it hinges upon the effective use of the protocols at the Step Two juncture, that is, bearing in mind writers' goals and issues while reading. Teacher modeling and practicing with milestone checks, reflection, and listening in whole-group settings are key to successful implementation of this part of the Step Two protocol for responders.

Step Two for the responders will always take some training, and a number of aids are included to assist teachers in this important undertaking. The third appendix to this chapter, Lesson 6C, teaches these listening protocols. In Part III, the **Peer Feedback Checklist (No. 7)**, the **Responder Reflection Organizer (No. 13)**, the **Active Listening Checklist (No. 6)**, and the **Good Listening Rubric (No. 16)** are all designed to aid students in active listening.

TEACHING TIPS FOR STEP TWO

- Run practice sessions on listening, instructing one partner to speak to the other for an allotted time period (usually 2 to 3 minutes). Instruct listeners to remember as much as possible about what was said. Assign a personal speaking topic like "Everything about yourself you can say in three minutes or less" or "Everything you can say about your favorite movie or book in two minutes." Repeat this process several times, and by the third or fourth try, students will develop effective listening strategies to remember the information. Discuss these strategies with them. Write them down on chart paper, and leave them up for continued reference and review.
- Provide students with lots of practice opportunities in one-on-one active listening sessions. Select two or three items from the **Active Listening Checklist** or the **Good Listening Rubric,** and develop a practice session around them. Write the short practice sessions on note cards, mix them up in a hat, and have students in buddy sessions select one card to practice with. For example, the sixth part on the **Active Listening Checklist,** "Nod when you hear something you like or agree with, but do not shake your head when you hear something you don't," can be coupled with the seventh part, "Pay attention to the speaker's body language—what isn't said often speaks louder than what is." While one student reads something persuasive (something generically written or taken from text), the other will listen and practice nodding in agreement when something is said that she or he agrees with. The student that reads will then report back what his or her interpretation of the listener's body language was, for example, saying, "You agreed with . . ." or "You didn't agree with . . ."
- Encouraging students to write down their thoughts while listening will help those with difficulty in short-term recall, but for other students, this strategy might preclude them from listening effectively simply because they can't do two things at the same time! Therefore, introduce students to each method and let them decide which is most effective for them. Instruct students to speak their thoughts to a peer partner *immediately* after the listening session without completing the **Peer Feedback Checklist** while listening. Then in another session, have them take notes on the **Peer Feedback Checklist** while writers read, completing it before offering any feedback. Discuss (1) which strategy works best to help them give good feedback and (2) how they can take notes and listen at the same time.

As a quick reference for teachers implementing this peer-coaching program, Figure 6.1 provides a brief listing of the forms used for completing Step Two by each of the student roles.

Figure 6.1   Forms for Executing Step Two

Writer	Responder
• Self-Feedback Checklist (No. 8) • Writer Summary Organizer (No. 14) • Oral Reading Rubric (No. 15)	• Active Listening Checklist (No. 6) • Good Listening Rubric (No. 16) • Peer Feedback Checklist (No. 7)
Editor	Manager
• Editor's Before Coaching Checklist (No. 9) • Editor's After and Between Coaching Checklist (No. 10) • Editor's Final Checklist and Rubric (No. 11)	• Manager's Checklist (No. 17)

APPENDIXES TO CHAPTER 6

Step Two for the Writer

Model Lesson 6A: Summarizing the Writing Piece

Model Lesson 6B: Reading Aloud for Feedback

Model Lesson 6C: Active Listening for the Feedback Selection

MODEL LESSON 6A

Step Two for the Writer: Summarizing the Writing Piece

Step: Step Two—Summarize and read.

Role: Writer

Content Area: Writing in all content areas

Skills: Summarizing, paraphrasing, identifying main idea, prewriting

Protocols:

Summarize your writing in one minute or less.

Read your piece aloud to the responder.

Lesson Time: 20 to 30 minutes

Materials/Forms Needed:

- **Writer Summary Organizer (No. 14)**
- **Steps and Guidelines for Writer (No. 31)** poster
- Highlighter pens
- Draft from previous peer-coaching sessions
- Projection device

Lesson/Student Objectives:

- Students will be primed for and prepared to execute their roles in the summary stages of Step Two as writer.
- Students will be able to cull the most relevant aspects of a writing piece to formulate a brief summary.
- Students will be able to complete the **Writer Summary Organizer (No. 14)** in preparation for writing their summary.
- Students will be able to summarize their writing piece for presentation to a peer or group of peers for peer coaching.

Lesson Summary: A brief discussion will ensue about the kinds of information contained in a summary, for example, establishing prior knowledge, main idea, important details, and information on characters. Following, the teacher will instruct students to highlight summary details in their individual writing pieces. Next, students will be directed to the **Writer Summary Organizer**. For student viewing, the teacher will project his or her own writing piece with summary details highlighted. A blank version of the **Writer Summary Organizer** will be placed up for viewing while students keep their copies on their desks. Using the **Writer Summary Organizer**, the teacher will demonstrate how the highlighted information is moved from a draft into a summary. Students watch the process and ask questions.

Steps for Administration:

1. Review Step 2 on the **Steps and Guidelines for Writer (No. 31)** poster, emphasizing the importance and placement of the summary of a writing piece.

2. Initiate a brief discussion about the type of information contained in a summary (establishing prior knowledge, main idea, important details, characters).

3. Instruct students to highlight similar summary information in their writing piece.

4. Place your own writing piece on an overhead projector or projection device, highlighting summary information while students watch.

5. Demonstrate how highlighted information is moved into a summary. One side will be the teacher's draft with highlighted summary details; the other side is a Summary Organizer.

    a. Tell students that you are going to create a summary using the details you highlighted, and that is how they should do it too.

    b. Think aloud as you work, allowing students to hear your thinking process.

6. When finished with highlighting and producing the summary draft, project a copy of your **Writer Summary Organizer** with relevant sections completed and a blank sheet next to it. If students do not need the **Writer Summary Organizer**, move directly from highlighted information on the draft to a summary draft. In this case, demonstrate the transfer from **Writer Summary Organizer** to blank paper, which will become the summary draft.

7. Begin to transfer information from the **Writer Summary Organizer** onto the blank paper that will serve as an initial summary draft. Think aloud as you work, allowing students to hear your thinking.

8. Review each section of the **Writer Summary Organizer**, and demonstrate for students how this information transfers into a summary, the organizer on one side and the summary draft on the other.

Instruct students to complete their own **Writer Summary Organizer** by using their information and highlighted drafts to create a summary on separate paper. As above, if students have had prior instruction on writing summaries, skip the organizer and instruct them to transfer highlighted information directly into their summary drafts.

Intervention Modifications:

1. For students who do not have a draft started, and therefore cannot highlight any summary information, allow them to go directly to the **Writer Summary Organizer** and fill it out completely, beginning with the first part. Often, the ideas contained in the **Writer Summary Organizer** can be a catalyst to starting a draft. As these students have nothing to receive feedback on, direct them to begin their drafts using information *from* the **Writer Summary Organizer.**

2. Highlight information using the draft that results from completion of the **Writer Summary Organizer** and then transfer this information to a summary draft.

Second-Language Modifications:

1. Place students in pairs.

2. One partner will ask the questions on the **Writer Summary Organizer** of the other, one question at a time. The partner asking the question will fill in the answer.

3. Partners will switch and repeat the process.

4. If students have not yet produced a draft, follow the intervention modification steps above to produce a draft from the summary questions.

MODEL LESSON 6B

Step Two for the Writer: Reading Aloud for Feedback

Step: Step Two—Summarize and read.

Role: Writer

Content Area: Writing in all content areas

Skills: Presentation, persuasion, oral speaking: expression, phrasing, intonation, timing, audience engagement

Protocol:

Read your piece aloud to the responder.

Lesson Time: 30 to 40 minutes

Materials Needed:

- **Steps and Guidelines for Writer (No. 31)** poster,
- **Oral Reading Rubric (No. 15)**
- Selected writing piece for oral reading or draft from previous sessions

Lesson/Student Objectives:

- Students will be prepared to read their writing piece aloud to peers for feedback.

- Students will be able to read to affect the tone and voice of their writing piece through prosody.

- Students will be able to project their voices to engage a wide range of listeners, thus adding to the tone and voice of their writing.

- Students will be able to enhance an effective message to the listener through eye contact, body language, and poise.

- Students will practice reading and presenting within an established time frame.

Lesson Summary: The teacher will model a reading from two different drafts (of the teacher's or another publication) and then receive feedback from students on it. Students will then practice reading aloud, using rubrics to critique each other for voice, tone, inflection, and overall audience engagement. Students will time each other to stay within an established time frame (one to three minutes, for example). If a student's piece is lengthy, that student may only be able to read the most salient portion of the entire piece.

Steps for Administration:

1. After reviewing the **Oral Reading Rubric (No. 15),** the teacher will read aloud while holding back on voice, tone, and pitch. To encourage evaluative judgment, the teacher will ask students what the reading sounded like.

2. Students will give feedback on the teacher's oral reading, using the **Oral Reading Rubric**.

3. In an attempt to improve the reading, the teacher will use feedback from the students to read the same writing piece again. When finished, the teacher will ask the students to compare the second reading to the first.

4. Students will rate the teacher's second reading on the **Oral Reading Rubric**, in pairs or individually.

5. A discussion will ensue about the rubric results, effective reading out loud, and oral reading relevance in the student peer-coaching process.

6. After teacher modeling and follow-up discussion, students will group into pairs to practice reading their pieces aloud to each other.

7. While one student reads, the other will rate the reading on the rubric, and then they will hold a discussion about the reading and rubric results; the students' discussion should be similar to the discussion that followed the teacher's modeling.

8. After two or three rounds of alternately reading their pieces aloud and reviewing their partners' readings, students will be ready to read aloud in their peer-coaching sessions.

Intervention Modifications:

1. Allow students additional (or unlimited when necessary) rounds of practice in reading, critiquing with the rubric, discussing, making adjustments, and reading again. Move the students into regular peer-coaching sessions only when they feel comfortable.

2. Refrain from their rating each other using the **Oral Reading Rubric**—keep feedback focused on their oral reading generally until students experiencing difficulty feel confident about their reading aloud. Then, and only then, you can introduce rating.

3. Introduce rating by having them rate themselves, or self-rate, after reading aloud (use taped readings of themselves when possible).

Second-Language Modifications:

1. Tape-record individual student readings, and let students use the rubric to make necessary adjustments to their own reading, repeating the process for ongoing practice.

2. Allow students to listen to and rate themselves before rating each other.

3. When students are confident and comfortable with self-rating, use the **Oral Reading Rubric**, allowing them to rate each other.

4. Allow students as many practice rounds as are needed for reading, reviewing, and self-rating using taped readings.

MODEL LESSON 6C

Step Two for the Responder: Active Listening for the Feedback Selection

Note: With modifications indicated, this lesson may also be used to prepare for silent peer-coaching sessions.

Step: Step Two—Listen to the piece as it is read (listening with a purpose).

Role: Responders

Content Area: Writing in all content areas

Skills: Active listening, verbal articulation, problem solving, critical analysis, reflection, determining author's message

Protocols:

Listen to provide feedback.

Employ active listening.

Lesson Time: 50 to 60 minutes

Materials/Forms Needed:

- **Role Descriptor Cards (No. 30)**
- **Steps and Guidelines for Responder (No. 32)** poster
- **Active Listening Checklist (No. 36)** poster
- **Peer Feedback Checklist (No. 7)**
- **Responder Reflection Organizer (No. 13)**
- **Writer Reflection Organizer (No. 12)**
- **Good Listening Rubric (No. 16)**
- Student writing piece
- Projection device

Lesson/Student Objectives:

- Students will be primed for and prepared to execute their roles as responders by effectively using active-listening skills.

- Students will be able to record effective listening notes on the **Peer Feedback Checklist (No. 7)**, considering what the writer asked for in feedback.

- Students will be able to listen effectively for the writer's goals as they are reflected in the writing piece.

- Students will respond with feedback focused on what the writer asked for, with consideration of the writer's goals, issues, and feedback type.

Lesson Summary: After the teacher engages students in establishing an issue for their own writing, a discussion will ensue about the role of the responder as an active listener; this discussion positions students for understanding how to listen for an issue, goal, and feedback choice. The teacher will review active-listening attributes from the **Active Listening Checklist (No. 36)** poster, (When using silent peer coaching, the teacher will discuss note taking and the use of the forms for active reading.) Students will practice the process of articulating issues and goals, reading the writing piece, listening, and responding on the **Responder Reflection Organizer (No. 13)** and then the **Peer Feedback Checklist** to clarify and articulate feedback. (Silent peer coaching will involve using the same forms, Nos. 7 and 13.) Some students may need to practice for several rounds before feedback is clarified. Finally, students will rate each other's progress using the **Good Listening Rubric (No. 16)**.

Steps for Administration:

1. Begin with 10 to 20 minutes of silent writing unless students have a prepared writing piece to use.

2. Remind students about the steps within both the writer and responder roles. Review the attributes of active listening printed on the **Active Listening Checklist** poster. (When silent peer coaching, discuss note taking and the use of the forms.)

- Ask for volunteers to recite the steps and attributes to you first, one at a time per volunteer.
- Review them together using the wall posters.
- Remind them that the posters are there to be referred to when needed.
- Hand out the writer and listener role cards; instruct students to read over their roles.

3. After reviewing the above, tell the students that you would like their feedback on something. Begin with something simple—like how the last lesson went for them or how they like peer-coaching sessions so far.

4. Tell them what your issue is in this feedback session; it should be something you are struggling with (for example, helping all students at the same time—they'll relate to this because they know they all want help at the same time!). Give them a summary of what has been done so far.

5. Next, ask students for a feedback type, such as "I heard . . ." feedback, on the issue. Ask them to first say something they liked using an "I liked . . ." statement, and then say what they can suggest for your issue. Remind them to use their **Peer Feedback Checklist**.

6. Field student responses. If silent peer coaching, have students write them down. Explain that they'll need to review the writer's **Goals List (No. 1)**.

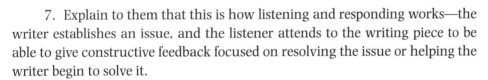

7. Explain to them that this is how listening and responding works—the writer establishes an issue, and the listener attends to the writing piece to be able to give constructive feedback focused on resolving the issue or helping the writer begin to solve it.

8. Place the **Good Listening Rubric** on a projection device for viewing by all and then collaboratively evaluate the students' feedback responses while teaching them how to navigate and use the rubric.

9. Using today's drafts, direct students to find a partner and read for buddy coaching—one is writer, the other is listener.

- Writers tell their goals and issues to their partners (refer students to their **Goals Lists**). Listeners record goals on the **Peer Feedback Checklist** form.
- If using the silent peer-coaching method, the writer will record goals and issues on a matrix, with the goals on one side and the issues on the other.
- The responder takes notes on the **Peer Feedback Checklist** while the writer reads.
- If using the silent peer-coaching method, the responder will first need to read the writer's writing piece silently and then take notes on the **Peer Feedback Checklist** during or immediately after reading.

10. When the writers have finished reading, bring the students' attention to a projected copy of the **Responder Reflection Organizer**.

11. Prompt students through each section.

- Some students may have been filling it out while the writer was reading, in which case they should complete it.
- You might say, *"Think about what you liked the most, and write it down. Next, think about what you heard in the writing that sounded like the goal was being met, or something that had to do with the issue. Write them down in the next box. For example, think about what you liked . . . Did you hear the details the writer asked for help with, and if not, where might they go? Did you hear vocabulary that helped you visualize a picture? Did you hear an author's unique voice?"*

12. One at a time, review each area on the **Responder Reflection Organizer**, checking off and reviewing each section.

13. Instruct students to read their **Responder Reflection Organizer** once before filling out the **Peer Feedback Checklist** to formulate their responses.

14. Buddy students up to communicate feedback.

- Remind them to first use their "I liked . . ." statements, followed by at least one "I heard . . ." statement, and then any suggestions for feedback.
- Students who are silent peer coaching will convey these statements through writing on a matrix working back and forth.

15. After receiving feedback, writers will use the **Writer Reflection Organizer (No. 12)** to reflect on the feedback. At this point, introduce the concept of an editor.

16. Hand out a *double-sided* copy of the **Good Listening Rubric** to each student. Instruct students to evaluate themselves and/or each other on their active listening participation.

17. Hold a class debriefing discussion on the process. Talk about what was easy, what may have been confusing, how the forms worked out, and whether feedback was helpful. Answer any questions students may have.

Intervention Modifications:

Some students may need the writing piece read a second and even a third time. When this is the case, allow them to continue working with their partner, rereading their piece and listening, then refining their responses on both the reflection sheet and checklist as needed. Circulate and offer assistance with targeting and positioning feedback responses to encourage them to be productive.

Second-Language Modifications:

Allow students to read, listen, and refine their responses on the forms as many times as needed until they are able to articulate responses with understanding and clarity.

7

Step Three

Giving and Using Feedback

> *Not every student is enthusiastic about giving helpful and detailed feedback to a partner. Quite often, middle-school students feel that honest feedback might cause them to lose friends. If students repeatedly resist providing helpful feedback to peers, get tough.*
>
> —Laura Robb, *Easy-to-Manage Reading & Writing Conferences*

STEP THREE FOR THE RESPONDER
GIVE FEEDBACK TO THE WRITER

The feedback process begins after student writers articulate their needs to the responders and responders position themselves for effective listening. Step Three for the responder contains the communication protocols necessary to ensure feedback is focused, appropriate, and what the writer asked for. The writer will then need to leverage this feedback with her or his goals, issues, and what he or she feels will work within the writing piece. Only writers can make these decisions, and this leveraging forces them to think the process through carefully.

Instruct students to

- Say what they liked best using "I liked . . ." followed by "I heard . . ." statements;
- Offer feedback focused on what the writer asked for; and
- *Not* use the word *you* in a statement unless it is a question or in an "I liked . . ." phrase.

Lifted out of an actual teaching session, the transcript that follows illustrates how students can become skilled in working with the language and skills of the peer-coaching process and how we'll need to coach and remind them along the way. These two high school students, both in Grade 12, are writing an essay about graduating and going to college. It is their first experience in peer coaching and their third session, having previously practiced setting goals and identifying issues in their writing. Wade indicated he typically struggles with his conclusions, and Matt indicated he has trouble staying on topic and maintaining focus in his writing. They know the feedback choices. Wade's goal is to write a good conclusion, and he selected "I heard . . ." feedback.

Note Matt's use of "I heard . . ." statements in his first response to Wade's writing. When prompted by the teacher to make suggestions, Matt became more specific by suggesting (albeit using the word *you*) that Wade place emotion in his conclusion as a method for resolving his stated issue (writing conclusions).

Student Transcript—Feedback Session

Matt: I heard how you put your emotion in there. I heard how you compared everything with something else, one side then another side to it.

Teacher: Any suggestions? Remember, Wade wanted "I heard . . ." feedback.

Wade: Yes, suggestions are OK.

Matt: When you write a conclusion, you might want to put the emotion from the middle into the end, so he could end it that way. (Matt forgot to leave out *you,* and we discussed briefly afterward the alternatives to using *you.*)

Teacher: Thanks, Matt; that was great. It sounds like Matt is suggesting that revisiting other parts of the essay before writing the conclusion is helpful. This is what I usually do when I am ready to write a conclusion. (Matt nods in agreement.)

Wade: Cool. Thanks.

In Step Three, readers respond to the author's stated needs using specific, objective beginning prompts, starting with a positive "I liked . . ." statement, telling what they liked best, followed by feedback in response to what writers say they want or need, using "I heard . . ." statements. After the "I heard . . ." statements, students may use any other "I" statement to express what they visualized, felt, or heard in the piece. Using prompts like "I suggest . . . ," "I might want to try . . . ," and "I would . . ." while refraining from the use of *you* statements prevents writers from personalizing feedback, while the responders retain ownership of their thoughts and opinions relative to the writing piece. This also allows the writers freedom to accept useful feedback and reject feedback that doesn't help them.

> I would not pay attention to feedback, and now I give good feedback and good descriptive feedback.
>
> (Hector Cordero, Grade 9)

Figure 7.1 provides sample language that can be used for helping students choose appropriate language for the Step Three protocols.

Figure 7.1   Script for Getting Students Started in Step Three

1. First, state what you liked best about the piece using an "I liked . . ." statement.

2. Next, state something positive about what you heard in the writing piece using "I heard . . ." statements.

3. Finally, state your suggestions for what the writer needs help with, still using "I" statements. Suggested prompts: "I suggest . . . ," "I might want to try . . . ," "I would . . . ," "I'd like to see . . . ," and "I have tried . . ."

Advanced Feedback: Peer Coaching as Questioning

Discussed fully in Chapter 4, peer coaching as questioning forces students to think about their writing on a deeper level, resulting in direct (and sometimes forced) reflection and analysis. In advanced sessions, writers can respond back to responders with questions—much as in the game *Jeopardy!* Figure 7.2 presents feedback used in both stating and questioning methods to make clear the contrasting effect on the writer. Generally, when presenting feedback as statements, responders help to improve or change content by giving specific suggestions for change: for example, "I might want to try describing the physical appearance of your mother." When presenting the feedback as questions, the thinking required for changing content is placed on writers; that is, instead of the previous statement, the responder might say, "How can you help me to know more about your mother?" Now, the writer needs to come up with ways to answer that question.

Figure 7.2 Feedback Statements for Goals and Issues

Stated Goal or Issue	Peer Feedback Statements	Peer Coaching as Questioning
Goal for persuasive essay (9th-grade student): *I want this to make people think about global warming and want to take action.* Peer coaching as questioning: *Does this essay make you think about global warming and want to take action?*	Student 1: *I like how you grab the reader from the beginning. Maybe you could scare them a little more with some more information about some of the local effects of global warming, like flooding, tornadoes in mountainous areas, etc.* Student 2: *I like the way it sounds because it sounds like you're talking right to the person face-to-face. Maybe it can be jazzed up a little bit by getting a little "in your face" with them about it—maybe use scarier words to do that; say things that might scare them into being more aware of the environment and global warming.* Writer: *Like what?* Student 2: *Like telling them about how long it takes for a diaper to biodegrade, or a piece of plastic. Or, I might talk about some of the whacky weather things that have been going on, like tornadoes and earthquakes.*	Student 1 ("I liked . . ." statement remains the same): *What could you do or say to scare them into being more conscientious?* Student 2 ("I liked . . ." statement remains the same): *What can you say or write to get in their face about it so that they get scared into doing something? What kind of reality check can you give them?*
Issue on a poem (7th-grade student): *I don't usually write poems, and I want to give this to my mom for Mother's Day, but I don't want her to feel bad after reading it. It's about a fight we had once, but it ended up OK.* (The goal for this student's piece was to write a poem that made her mother feel happy inside.) Peer coaching as questioning: *Do you think my mom will like this poem and feel good about it even though it talks about a fight we had once?*	*I hear someone talking to their mother in this poem. Words like* Pretty Woman *and* Always Everything *make her sound very special. If I were a mom, I would not feel bad because it is more about that she is loved than about the fight. The fight sounds real from "red-faced girl with bulging eyes." To make someone not feel bad about remembering a fight, maybe leave out some detail. I know we're always supposed to use detail, but this time leave it out there and maybe add some more in the loving spots.*	*If there were some detail that might bug your mom, what would you leave out? What detail makes you feel the most apprehensive, and would the poem still work if you left it out?*
Goal (6th-grade student): *I want to write a historical fiction story and maybe make it into a novel.* Peer coaching as questioning: *How can I make this short story into a novel?*	*I like how the character starts talking right away, and she's another kind of slave from a country other than Africa, going back far in time—that's really interesting! I didn't know they had slaves in other countries. I would make this longer, into a novel, by having her tell about how she got there in the first place and then writing about all the things that happened to her before becoming a slave. Maybe have her writing it in her diary.*	("I liked . . ." statement remains the same.) *How can the main character tell her whole life enough to make a longer story? What would she need to include? What might she use to do it?*

As can be seen in the exchanges in Figure 7.2, I had to adjust the original language and coach students heavily in the Peer Feedback Statements column to leave out the *you* statements. At first, students will need constant reminding on this, but it really does work to offset the personal, and they're much more motivated to incorporate changes when they are not explicitly told to do so. The Peer Coaching as Questioning column allows for more use of *you* because feedback is in the form of questions, not directives.

TEACHING TIPS FOR STEP THREE (RESPONDER)

- Use of "I" statements versus "You should" statements will work to offset any negative feedback (even if the negativity is only perceptual on the part of the writers), over-personalization, or perceived directives, encouraging students to make changes. Practice with these statements in multiple settings across content areas as opportunities present themselves, such as prereading activities before writing about personal experiences, responding to text, and journal responses.
- Facilitate the transition of using *"I heard..."* or *"I felt..."* versus "You should..." or "You ought to..." when students are interacting with one another by having them write down in their journals every time they use, or almost use, a "you" statement and replace it with an "I" statement. Stress that old habits take time to break and replace with new ways of behaving; initiate a group discussion about this type of communication using the following prompts: "Why is it better to use 'I' statements?" "What happens when we don't?" "Why should we not use *you?*"
- Review all Step Three ancillary materials regularly, particularly the **Peer Feedback Checklist (No. 7)**, the **Writer Reflection Organizer (No. 12)**, and the **Responder Reflection Organizer (No. 13)**, to revisit goals, issues, and feedback requests so that feedback remains relevant and focused.

Below is another transcript of a group that is just beginning to learn the process. The teacher, in this instance myself, typifies how we need to constantly monitor the use of "I" statements.

Responder:	It's boring.
Teacher:	Instead of saying it's boring, let's think about saying it so that it's productive. Remember those feedback statements we practiced with? (Points to chart paper with brainstormed statements/prompts written on it.)
Another student in the group:	Yeah! He forgot to say "I liked . . ." too.
Teacher:	First, how can we rephrase it? Which prompt should we use?
Responder:	I heard . . . No, I didn't hear . . .
Teacher:	No, it has to be an "I heard . . ." statement.

Responder:	OK . . . I heard that there might be room for some more action in the beginning after the motorcycle part . . . Ummm . . . maybe rides and stuff, and description.
Teacher:	Can you think of a specific thing he can describe? Use your "I" statements. Try to stay away from "you" statements.
Responder:	I would put like, how to play basketball, and what we did.
Responder 2:	I heard that he loves it. I can sense it, that he likes it.

STEP THREE FOR THE WRITER
DECIDE WHAT FEEDBACK TO USE

- *Take what you need (in feedback), and leave out what you do not.*
- *Make adjustments to your writing.*

Only writers can decide what feedback to use; making these decisions will require a careful review and analysis of their goals, issues set, and feedback asked for as well as bearing in mind the feedback received. Reconciling all of this information with what writers need and where they want to end up in their writing is a taxing effort, but an attainable objective. Three resources provided by this program, the **Peer Feedback Checklist (No. 7)** for the responder; the editor checklists, **Editor's Before Coaching Checklist (No. 9)**, **Editor's After and Between Coaching Checklist (No. 10)**, and **Editor's Final Checklist and Rubric (No. 11)**; and the **Writer Reflection Organizer (No. 12)** and **Responder Reflection Organizer (No. 13)**, will provide students with materials that assist them in reflecting upon and analyzing their work. While these documents are aiding them in making these decisions, the writers are transitioning into automatic and independent use of the protocols. Model Lesson 7A, Articulating Feedback to the Writer, teaches these protocols and is placed at the end of this chapter. The following self-questions facilitate an effective think-through process until students can apply it independently.

- Have I looked back at my goals and made sure that the feedback focuses on what I asked for from my peers?
- Did I reflect on these goals and feedback requests?
- Did I use the **Writer Reflection Organizer** to reflect on my goals and issues and this feedback?
- What parts of the feedback work into my goal for the writing piece?
- Does the feedback also focus on the project or assignment goals as set by the teacher?
- Did I check my **Feedback Type Checklist** to be sure that what I asked for was provided in the feedback? Did I include everything? Do I need to change anything?
- What parts of the feedback address the issues I needed help with?
- What part of the feedback works within my personal writing style?
- What part of the feedback will help make my writing better, awesome, and its ultimate best?

Responders have the responsibility for answering the writers' calls for feedback on goals, issues, general feedback, or no feedback. Writers have the even greater responsibility for deciding what to do with that feedback. This collaborative process can be a powerful tool in the growth of student writing ability.

TEACHING TIPS FOR STEP THREE (WRITER)

- Model the feedback decision-making process by thinking out loud about a personal writing piece. Use a teacher-generated writing sample or another generic writing piece, and place it where all can view it while you're thinking aloud. Don't hold back—discuss any reservations, struggles within the writing, and frustrations. Let your students hear your ideas as they enter your head.
- Use a similar think-through process that models for students how a decision was arrived at—what was considered, how it aligned with the piece's goals or issues stated, and what is worthy of further development.

Student Example From Transcript Above

Wade struggled with his conclusion as a result of struggling with the process of writing in general—getting started with ideas and keeping them flowing. Below are before and after examples of Wade's writing, demonstrating how the feedback in three peer-coaching sessions worked to resolve his writing issue and produce a better piece of writing.

Wade's Goals:

1. I would like for this writing to be published.

2. I would like for this writing to be truthful.

3. I want to accomplish helping with this project.

Wade's Issue:

I feel that I can write good conclusions, but the process takes me too long. I really have to sit with it and think about what I want to say. It doesn't come as natural as the rest of the essay.

Wade's Draft Conclusion:

High school has been an experience that I will value and treasure forever. However, in a couple months when I am signing my friend's yearbooks and everyone is writing about how excited they are for the future, realize this: there are many students just like me who are equally nervous and anxious for school to start as excited.

Feedback to Wade From Matt, His Peer Coach:

When you write a conclusion, you might want to put the emotion from the middle into the end, so he could end it that way.

Wade's Final Conclusion, After the Third Round of Peer Coaching:

My high school years have been an experience that I will value and treasure forever. However, as with anything else with a beginning, it must come to an end. Fortunately, this is the beginning of something I believe will exceed the experience of high school, and do more for my future. College is the next chapter in my book of life, and I am nervous, anxious, and excited to turn the page.

Commentary: Note how Wade responded to Matt's encouragement of placing "the emotion from the middle into the end" with Wade's ending statement: "I am nervous, anxious, and excited to turn the page." What a powerful ending, one that most seniors would relate to.

To assist you in identifying the forms needed for Step Three, Figure 7.3 provides a guide in the use of forms for each role.

Figure 7.3   Forms for Executing Step Three

Writer	Responder
• Self-Feedback Checklist (No. 8) • Writer Reflection Organizer (No. 12)	• Peer Feedback Checklist (No. 7) • Responder Reflection Organizer (No. 13)
Editor	Manager
• Editor's After and Between Coaching Checklist (No. 10) • Editor's Final Checklist and Rubric (No. 11)	• Manager's Checklist (No. 17)

APPENDIXES TO CHAPTER 7

Step Three for the Responder

Model Lesson 7A: Articulating Feedback to the Writer—Actionable Versus General

Model Lesson 7B: Incorporating Feedback Into the Writing

MODEL LESSON 7A

Step Three for the Responder: Articulating Feedback to the Writer—Actionable Versus General

Note: This lesson may also be used to prepare for silent peer-coaching sessions.

Step: Step Three—Give feedback to the writer.

Role: Responder

Content Area: Writing in all content areas

Skills: Communication, peer review, effective listening, verbal articulation, speaking, recognizing cause/effect in speaking, decision making, problem solving, distinguishing between actionable versus vague or general feedback, comparing/contrasting

Protocols:

First, *say what you liked best using "I liked . . ." and/or "I heard . . ." statements.*

Next, *offer feedback focused on what the writer asked for.*

Lesson Time: 30 to 40 minutes

Materials:

- **Steps and Guidelines for Writer (No. 31)** poster
- **Steps and Guidelines for Responder (No. 32)** poster
- **Responder Reflection Organizer (No. 13)**
- **Peer Feedback Checklist (No. 7)**

Lesson/Student Objectives:

- Students will understand the differences in and results of the language alternatives, which can be used in requests or in communication of ideas.
- Writers will understand the impact of an affirmative "I want . . ." or "I need . . ." statement in obtaining help and eliciting cooperation from peers.

- Responders will understand the positive impact of an "I liked . . ." statement immediately following a reading versus "You should . . ." statements.
- Responders will understand the impact and objectivity of "I heard . . ." statements.
- Responders will understand why "you" is only used in a question or in "I liked . . ." statements in feedback.
- Writers and responders will effectively articulate productive give-and-take in the feedback sessions by engaging in productive conversations about their writing.

Lesson Summary: The teacher will discuss the reasoning behind using the "I liked . . ." and "I heard . . ." statements when offering feedback as well as explaining the importance of avoiding the use of the word *you*. A discussion will follow on how to use the prompts most effectively. Through brainstorming, students will propose alternate responses to hypothetical feedback statements such as "I didn't like . . ." and "It should have said . . ." Students will also discuss reactions to each response and how these reactions may vary. In the second phase of the class, students will discuss the differences between *general* feedback and *actionable* feedback, using a similar brainstorm compare/contrast process. After understanding is gained, students will practice responding to each other by reading segments from their drafts in pairs, while the teacher circulates and coaches them, reminding them of the protocols.

Steps for Administration:

First Phase

1. Review the steps for writers on the **Steps and Guidelines for Writer (No. 31)** poster. Emphasize the following protocols in Step One:

   a. *"I heard . . ." feedback only* (what peer coaching buddies heard).

   b. Ask students, "Why is it important to use 'I heard . . .' rather than statements like 'You should . . .' or 'It didn't . . .'?"

   c. Review the steps for responders on the **Steps and Guidelines for Responder (No. 32)** poster, and the "I liked . . ." and "I heard . . ." statements on the **Peer Feedback Checklist (No. 7)**. Point out Step Three on the poster: *After listening to the writer read aloud, respond with feedback: First, say what you liked best using "I liked . . ." followed by "I heard . . ." statements. Next, offer feedback focused on what the writer asked for.*

   d. Ask students why it is better to first say what you liked, and then tell the writer what you heard.

2. Develop a matrix similar to the one in Figure 7.4 demonstrating how a particular statement can produce one result, while a different statement can produce a much different result.

Figure 7.4   Statement and Reaction (Cause/Effect) Matrix

Statement		Reaction
Cause		Effect

I liked how you . . .	Ask students how one statement would make them feel versus the other.	Writer feels good.
It shouldn't have so much talking.		I don't think I want to write any more.
I heard a lot of good dialogue and description.		I think I'll keep doing what I was doing then.
I might try using more adjectives to add to that nice description.		It needs more adjectives. That's a good idea; I'll add more adjectives.

Second Phase

3. To demonstrate the difference in feedback responses, select a student volunteer to work with.

4. Provide the student with a writing draft to read from, or ask the student to read from his or her own draft.

5. First, give vague feedback: "I like the way it flowed" or "It was good." Use a couple of *you* statements, such as "I didn't like how you . . ." or "You should . . ."

6. Conduct a similar activity with a few more student volunteers.

7. Discuss with the volunteers how it felt to receive that feedback or how they think they would feel if they were the writer. Reinforce the reasoning behind the protocols of "I liked . . . ," "I heard . . . ," and avoiding "you . . ."

8. Discuss alternatives, and repeat the process but respond with different feedback statements using the protocol: "I liked how . . . ," "I heard that . . . ," and "I might try . . ."

9. After the teacher modeling session above, discuss alternative feedback statements using a compare/contrast matrix first focusing on positive versus negative, then on actionable versus general, such as in Figures 7.5 and 7.6.

Figure 7.5   Positive Versus Negative Feedback Statements

Positive	Negative
I liked the title.	The only part of it I liked is the title.
The title was interesting, but I might want to focus on . . . (Or, I might want to look at . . .)	You didn't make the title fit, and it made it confusing.
I heard the focus ideas and supporting evidence, but I had trouble understanding. Maybe a thesis statement would help.	I didn't hear a thesis statement, and without one, it will get an F. You need to write a thesis statement.

Figure 7.6   Actionable Versus General Feedback Statements

Actionable	General
I heard a lot of adjectives that sounded like a writer's voice.	It sounded OK. Teacher: *What sounded OK about it?*
I like the organization and the argument—it makes it interesting.	I liked the way it sounded all through. Teacher: *What did you like about it? What worked the best?*
Have you tried thinking of a title *before* beginning writing? I might title it . . .	You should title your work first. Teacher: *What might a good title be?*

10. Buddy students up for practice in responding to one another, with one student reading a segment from a writing piece, the other responding verbally, using appropriate statements.

11. Circulate to coach and gently remind them that breaking an old habit and building a new one takes time and practice.

Intervention Modifications:

1. Give students a blank matrix and have them brainstorm with partners' feedback statements on both sides—one side actionable, the other general. Do this for both feedback requests and feedback statements.

2. Ask students to write down how they feel after each feedback type and discuss these differences in small groups or with a peer.

3. Allow students who need additional support in culling "I liked . . ." and "I heard . . ." statements to read and highlight the writing piece, or a copy of the writing piece, to encourage them to visually identify what they liked and what they heard before practicing giving feedback.

Second-Language Modifications:

1. Work students through the prompts on the **Peer Feedback Checklist** and the **Steps and Guidelines for Writer** and **Steps and Guidelines for Responder** posters.

2. Hand out cards with goals and issues written on them, such as "I want . . . ," "I heard . . ." feedback only, or "My goal is to make my parents proud" or "My goal is to finish." (Actual student goals may be used anonymously.)

3. Direct students to write an actionable feedback statement on the matrix in response to the prompts on the cards.

4. Read aloud a short passage from a student's work or a published work to help students practice "I heard . . ." statements. Using a blank matrix, instruct students to write "I heard . . ." statements on one side and insert an opposite statement on the other side.

5. In the middle of the matrix, write in the effects of each statement, and discuss them.

6. Allow statements to be broad at first, and then expand them with more focused vocabulary using the compare/contrast matrix. (This will require one-on-one conferring or partnering with a peer who has mastered the concept.) See Figure 7.7 for the Compare/Contrast Matrix for Feedback.

Figure 7.7   Compare/Contrast Matrix for Feedback

I liked Stanley's mom. *What did she do to make you like her?*	I liked the way Stanley's mom made him write. *What did she make him write? How did she make him?*
I liked the title. *What did you like about the title?*	I like how you name the fish in the title. *Is there a title you might give it?*
I liked how your introduction was described. *What did you like about the description?*	I like how the introduction described Abraham Lincoln as a boy. *What are some of the things it said about him as a boy?*

MODEL LESSON 7B

Step Three for the Writer: Incorporating Feedback Into the Writing

Note: This lesson may also be used to prepare for silent peer-coaching sessions.

Step: Step Three—Decide what feedback to use.

Roles: Writer, Editor

Content Area: Writing in all content areas

Skills: Decision making, problem solving, critical analysis, revising, editing

Protocols:

Take what you need (in feedback) and leave out what you do not.

Make adjustments to your writing.

Lesson Time: 30 to 40 minutes

Materials and Forms:

- **Steps and Guidelines for Writer (No. 31)** poster
- **List of Responsibilities for Editor (No. 34)** poster
- **Editor's After and Between Coaching Checklist (No. 10)**
- **Editor's Final Checklist and Rubric (No. 11)**
- **Self-Feedback Checklist (No. 8)**
- **Writer Reflection Organizer (No. 12)**
- Student writing draft

Lesson/Student Objectives:

- Students will be primed for and prepared to execute their roles as writer in the decision-making process about their writing.
- Student editors will aid the writer in deciding what feedback to use and in incorporating that feedback into the writing.
- Students will be able to decipher useful feedback from less-useful feedback as it applies to their writing piece.
- Students will be able to import useful feedback into their writing piece as part of the revision/rewriting process.

Lesson Summary: After referring students to the **Steps and Guidelines for Writer (No. 31)** poster to review Step Three, the teacher will demonstrate how he or she makes decisions on feedback using the **Writer Reflection Organizer (No. 12)** to reflect on feedback. After the teacher demonstrates a think-through process, students will be directed to review their own feedback and decide what they will be incorporating into their writing piece. Students will discuss these decisions with their editor and then revise the writing piece accordingly. (Editors will use the **Editor's After and Between Coaching Checklist (No. 10)** and the **Editor's Final Checklist and Rubric (No. 11)** to offer assistance.

Steps for Administration:

1. Refer students to the **Steps and Guidelines for Writer** to review Step Three:

Take what you need (in feedback) and leave out what you do not.

Make adjustments to your writing.

2. Tell students that you are going to demonstrate completion of the **Writer Reflection Organizer** for your own writing piece. Encourage them to listen as you think through the decision-making process aloud. Here are some examples of think-aloud statements:

   a. "Let's see . . . my goals were to make this piece longer and to be more persuasive."

   b. "This feedback on changing the ending isn't anything that applies to my goal or my issue."

   c. "It looks like the second suggestion on using detail might help me with my issue, which was that it was too short . . ."

3. Lead a brief discussion about Step Three of the writer's protocol; include points such as what factors into the decision-making process (goals and issues); and how the writer can tell when feedback is going to be useful, less useful, or not useful. Reinforce the concept that all feedback can be helpful but not always to a particular piece, especially if it doesn't apply to what was asked for. Sometimes feedback can be revisited. If it is not used when it is received, perhaps it will be useful another time.

4. Instruct students to review the feedback they received, using the **Writer Reflection Organizer**.

   a. When possible, have students review it with the peer who gave them the feedback.

   b. Use this buddy session as an opportunity to give assistance to those who are not able to decide which feedback to use.

5. Encourage students to use the **Self-Feedback Checklist (No. 8)** to help them decide what to use and what not to use. If students are unclear about feedback that may be vague or overly general yet possibly useful, allow them an opportunity to confer with the peer who made the suggestions.

6. Instruct students to incorporate the feedback they decide to use into their writing piece.

   a. Some students may need more detail on some specific feedback. When possible, allow them to seek clarification from the person who gave them the feedback.

   b. For students unable to use any of the feedback, have them attempt to self-coach by reading the piece silently and working it through on the **Self-Feedback Checklist**.

7. Students finishing before others may repeat the student peer-coaching process using their revised writing pieces.

Intervention Modifications:

1. Have one-on-one conferences with students struggling in the decision-making process. Talk them through each area on the **Self-Feedback Checklist** and the **Writer Reflection Organizer** to help them reconcile the feedback with their stated goals and issues.

2. Color highlight their goals and issues inside of the writing piece so that a direct connection between goals and feedback is evident.

3. Allow students extended time to consult with other students (editors and responders who gave them their feedback) on feedback—which to use, how to use it, and any other clarification they may need.

Second-Language Modifications:

1. In addition to the above, allow students extended time to work with more than one editor.

2. Use the **Editor's After and Between Coaching Checklist** to clarify feedback.

3. Allow students another opportunity to read their pieces aloud to the editor or another peer after first articulating their goals and issues.

4. Allow editors to serve in the role of responder, though with tighter oversight in the articulation and administering of feedback.

5. After receiving additional assistance or feedback from the editor, students can return to their seats to use any new feedback.

PART III

36 Reproducible Tools for Implementation and Assessment

1. Goals List (Step One) *

2. Goals List for Peer Coaching as Questioning (Step One) Ŧ

3. Identifying an Issue Checklist (Step One) *

4. Identifying an Issue for Peer Coaching as Questioning (Step One) Ŧ

5. Feedback Type Checklist: A Think-Through for the Writer (Step One) * Ŧ

6. Active Listening Checklist (Steps One and Two) Ŧ

7. Peer Feedback Checklist (Steps One, Two, and Three, Responder) * Ŧ

8. Self-Feedback Checklist (Steps Two and Three, Writer) *

9. Editor's Before Coaching Checklist Ŧ

10. Editor's After and Between Coaching Checklist (Steps One, Two, and Three)

11. Editor's Final Checklist and Rubric (Steps One, Two, and Three)

12. Writer Reflection Organizer (Step Three) * Ŧ

13. Responder Reflection Organizer (Step Three) * Ŧ

14. Writer Summary Organizer (Step Two) * Ŧ

15. Oral Reading Rubric (Step Two) Ŧ

16. Good Listening Rubric Ŧ

17. Manager's Checklist

18. Teacher Anecdotal Notes Record for Writers (Steps One, Two, and Three)

19. Teacher Anecdotal Notes Record for Responders (Steps One, Two, and Three)

20. Teacher Anecdotal Notes Record for Editors (Steps One, Two, and Three)

21. Teacher Anecdotal Notes Record for Managers (Steps One, Two, and Three)

22. Peer Role Evaluation Rubric for Writer

23. Peer Role Evaluation Rubric for Responder

24. Peer Role Evaluation Rubric for Editor

25. Peer Role Evaluation Rubric for Manager

26. Teacher Role Evaluation Rubric for Writer

27. Teacher Role Evaluation Rubric for Responder

28. Teacher Role Evaluation Rubric for Editor

29. Teacher Role Evaluation Rubric for Manager

30. Role Descriptor Cards

The following forms are meant to be used as posters, which you can copy and enlarge as needed to put up in the classroom for quick reference.

31. Steps and Guidelines for Writer

32. Steps and Guidelines for Responder

33. Feedback Choices for Writer

34. List of Responsibilities for Editor

35. List of Responsibilities for Manager

36. Active Listening Checklist

---

*Denotes those forms that can be used for silent peer coaching.

Ŧ Denotes those forms that can be used for peer coaching as questioning.

* Ŧ Indicates that a form can be used for both.

1. Goals List (Step One)

Name _____

    Because every draft is driven by a goal, and good goals make for good writing, use this check-list to help you decide what your goals will be for this draft. Begin by writing down some information about this draft:

Genre or assignment type: _____

Title (if known): _____

    1. **Project Goals (if applicable):** Think about the goals that your teacher set for this project, or the project's purpose. This will help you establish your goal or goals for this writing project. Write them down below (Examples: Finish introduction and thesis by Friday, write and describe three accomplishments of someone famous in the 19th century, write a persuasive essay about health care in America):

Project Goal 1:
Project Goal 2:

    2. **Write down three things you want this writing to do or to accomplish when finished** (Examples: get published, get an A, finish by Friday, make people think about the subject, make people take action, etc.):

a. _____

b. _____

c. _____

3. **Brainstorm:** Finish one or two of the following statements:

I want this draft to _____

With this draft, I want to _____

This writing will _____

4. **Now, write down your goal or goals for this writing project** (Examples: Write a strong introduction or conclusion, write more persuasively in the beginning to get attention, finish by Friday, use more detail, etc.):

Goal 1:
Goal 2:
Goal 2:

Congratulations! You've successfully completed Step One of peer coaching—identifying a goal or goals for your draft. Good work!

2. Goals List for Peer Coaching as Questioning (Step One)

Name _____

Because every draft is driven by a goal, and good goals make for good writing, use this sheet and list to help set some goals for your draft. **Responders may use this list to coach the writer in developing these goals by asking the questions below**, adding more if needed. Begin by writing down, or asking the writer for, some information about this draft:

1. **What is the genre or assignment type?** _____

What is the title, and why did you give it this title? Explain:

2. **Project Goals (where applicable):**

What were the teacher's goals for this project? (Ask the teacher if you need to.)
What is the project's purpose? (Ask the teacher if you need to.)

3. **What are three things you would like this writing to do or to accomplish when finished?** (Examples: get published, make my parents proud, get an A, enter it in a contest, get me a scholarship, etc.)

a. _____

b. _____

c. _____

4. **Brainstorm: Finish one or two of the following Goals Statements as a question:**

Goal Statement 1. *Why do I want this draft to* _____?

Goal Statement 2. *With this draft, will I* _____?

Goal Statement 3. *Will this piece* _____?

5. **Now, write down your goal or goals for this writing project *in the form of a question*:**

Goal 1:
Goal 2:
Goal 3:

Congratulations! You've successfully completed Step One of peer coaching—identifying a goal or goals for your draft. Good work!

3. Identifying an Issue Checklist (Step One)

Name _____

Check (✓) one genre:

    Fiction: ___ poem ___ story ___ novel ___ chapter ___ screenplay ___ other: _____

    Nonfiction: ___ autobiography ___ biography ___ essay ___ persuasive essay ___ other: _____

Check (✓) one subject:

    ___ language arts ___ math ___ science ___ social studies ___ art ___ other: _____

Before reading your piece aloud, follow these steps, using these options and prompts to help you decide **what you need help with**, and how to communicate this to the responder for helpful feedback.

Directions: Read your piece over carefully to decide what you are struggling with or need help with. Check off the areas that you know apply or that might apply as you continue to write.

    1. I need, or would like, some help in the following areas:

____ Introduction	____ Character names
____ Beginning	____ Time-order
____ Ending	____ Detail
____ Organization	____ Dialogue
____ Character	____ Completion
____ Repetition	____ Length
____ Rhyming	____ Other: _____

2. State why you checked what you did in Item 1, and provide as much detail as possible (if peer coaching as questioning, write in the form of a question).

_____

_____

_____

_____

_____

_____

_____

_____

_____

_____

_____

_____

_____

_____

_____

3. State clearly what you want help with, using "I" statements. Finish one of the statements (if peer coaching as questioning, finish in the form of a question):

- *I am having trouble with* _____
- *I need to know what you hear when* _____
- *I'm not sure about* _____
- *I want help with* _____

Congratulations! You've successfully identified something that you need help with, and you've communicated it to your fellow peer coaches. You're that much closer to making your writing better and to getting an A!

4. Identifying an Issue for Peer Coaching as Questioning (Step One)

Name _____

This checklist can be completed by either the writer or the responder to help writers decide what they need help with or what the issues are in the draft. Responders may also ask the questions to the writer to help him or her through the process.

Check (✔) one genre:

Fiction: ___ poem ___ story ___ novel ___ chapter ___ screenplay ___ other: _____

Non-fiction: ___ autobiography ___ biography ___essay ___ persuasive essay ___ other: _____

Check (✔) one subject:

___ language arts ___ math ___ science ___ social studies ___ art ___ other: _____

Directions: Read your draft over carefully and then ask and answer each question below before checking off all areas that apply.

1. I may want or need help with this draft in the following areas:

____ **Introduction/thesis:** *How does the introduction sound? Does this thesis statement capture the introduction and main ideas the project needs or that I need to make this good?*

____ **Time-order:** *Is there a sense for time period in this? Is it important to have that for this draft? Does the timeline flow in order?*

____ **Beginning:** *What made me want to begin it with this? How does it work as an introduction or a thesis statement?*

____ **Detail:** *Does every detail help the storyline? Are there enough details to persuade the reader?*

____ **Conclusion:** *Does it end the way I want it to end or have pictured it to end? Does it bring all other information around full circle?*

____ **Organization:** *Am I satisfied with the organizational structure, or can it be better organized? Where is it lacking?*

____ **Character development:** *Do the characters look and act the way I've been picturing and imagining them to?*

____ **Repetition:** *Does the poem use enough repetition to give it a strong feeling or voice? Is the draft too repetitive, or does it repeat itself in places?*

____ **Rhyming:** *Am I satisfied with the rhyming or does it sound like I tried too hard, or like it is contrived?*

____ **Dialogue:** *Is there enough talking among the characters, or should there be more? Do they sound like real people talking?*

____ **Argument/persuasion:** *Is the reader convinced of a position? Is my own position clear enough? Do I make the reader feel as passionately as the author?*

____ **Style:** *Am I satisfied with the writing style? Is the author's own writing style clear?*

____ **Length:** *Does it meet the length requirements of the teacher or project goal? Am I satisfied with how long (or short) it is?*

____ **Spelling/grammar/punctuation:** *How much more review will be needed in this area? Am I confident about the spelling and grammar?*

Explain any areas checked above—for example, why is the help needed, and how can it be given?

_____

_____

_____

_____

_____

2. State clearly what you want help with using "I" statements. Finish one of the questions:
   - *Am I having trouble with . . . ?*
   - *Do I need to know what you hear when . . . ?*
   - *Am I not sure about . . . ?*
   - *Do I want help with . . . ?*

Clarification questions *for* the writer: Write down any clarification questions the responder has for the writer:

Clarification questions from the writer: Write down any questions you have about your draft. Examples: What if I ended it differently? Is my beginning too strong? Did I add enough detail about the . . . ? Does my thesis statement sound OK?

Congratulations! You've successfully identified areas that you need help with, and you've communicated it to your fellow peer coaches through questioning. Good work!

5. Feedback Type Checklist: A Think-Through for the Writer (Step One)

Name _____

Use this guide to help you decide on a feedback option. These are your feedback choices:

1. Feedback on goals only

2. Feedback on issues only

3. Feedback on goals and issues

4. "I heard . . ." feedback only

5. No feedback (only available once)

1. **Check each one that applies to your draft:**

   ○ I am not sure if I can meet my own goal.

   ○ My goal is very similar to the project goal.

   ○ I have written no more than one paragraph or less.

   ○ This is my first draft—I do not have any goal yet.

If you placed a (✔) next to two or more above, you will want to select Item 1 for feedback—*Feedback on my goals only.*

2. **Check each one that applies to your draft:**

   ○ I've identified one or more issues for this draft.

   ○ My goals and issues are similar.

   ○ The project's goal won't be met unless my issue is resolved.

   ○ I can't finish this piece until my issue is resolved.

If you placed a (✔) next to one or more of the above, you will want to select option Item 2 or 3 for feedback—*feedback on issues only* or *feedback on goals and issues.*

3. **Check each one that applies to your draft:**

○ I have a goal for my draft, but
I have no issue yet.

○ I am not sure where I want to go
with this draft yet.

○ I do not have a goal established
for my draft yet.

○ I want to hear what other people have
to say about this draft.

If you placed a (✔) next to one or more of the above, you will want to select Item 4 for feedback—"I heard . . ." feedback only.

4. **Check each one that applies to your draft:**

○ This piece has *not* been read to a
partner or group for peer
coaching yet.

○ The "No Feedback" option has *not* been
exercised yet.

○ This is the first time for feedback
on this piece.

If you placed a (✔) next to any of the above, you may select option Item 5 for feedback—No feedback (only available once).

6. Active Listening Checklist (Steps One and Two)

Name _____

Use this checklist to guide your active listening. Remember: Active listening means excellent listening. Excellent listening results in remembering and giving the best feedback you can give to your peer-coaching partners.

1. Give the speaker your undivided attention.

    ⇒ Position your body toward the speaker and look directly at him or her.

    ⇒ Hands at your sides, on the desk, ready to take notes.

2. Keep the writer goals and issues out where you can see them as reminders for what to listen for.

3. Keep a note pad handy.

4. When any feedback comes to mind, write it down immediately.

5. No talking—talking and listening at the same time is impossible!

6. Nod when you hear something you like or agree with, but *do not* shake your head when you hear something you don't like or agree with.

7. Pay attention to the speaker's body language—what *isn't* said often speaks louder than what is said.

8. *Do not* give thoughts or distractions any more than 30 seconds—think immediately about the writer's goals and issues to bring yourself back to active listening.

9. Make small mental summaries of what is read to lock it into memory; picture yourself writing it down.

10. Ask questions when needed.

11. Visualize what the speaker is talking about by drawing a mental picture.

12. Do not interrupt the speaker with questions, feedback, or comments—wait until she or he is through reading.

Write down one or more goals, or areas you would like to improve on in active listening:

1. _____

2. _____

3. _____

---

7. Peer Feedback Checklist (Steps One, Two, and Three, Responder)

Name _____

Use this checklist after listening carefully to what the writer stated she or he needed help with before responding with feedback or suggestions. The following prompts will help you know what to listen for.

1. Indicate here what the writer's goal is for this draft:

   _____

2. Need/Issue/Suggestions: write down any issues the writer stated:

   _____

Check the writer's chosen feedback:

_____ Feedback on goals only   _____ "I heard . . ." feedback only

_____ Feedback on issues only   _____ No feedback (only available once)

_____ Feedback on goals and issues

3. Ask the writer any questions you have about the goal, the issue, or the feedback choice.

4. **After the writer reads**: State what you liked best about the piece using an "I liked . . ." statement. After the "I liked . . ." statement, make an "I heard . . ." statement. Here are some examples:

- I liked the way . . .

- I liked when . . .

- I liked it best when . . .

- I heard and saw a lot of . . .

- I heard how . . .

5. After stating what you liked best about the draft, fill out the Responder Reflection Organizer. Use some more statements to provide helpful suggestions for the writer. Here are some examples: "Has this been tried . . ." "If it were me, I might . . ." "I wanted to see (or hear) more . . ." "I might try . . ."

Figure F.1 shows some examples, and Figure F.2 shows what you might look for and respond to.

Figure F.1 Full Feedback Examples

Fiction: (This writer wanted help developing a stronger voice.) *I heard some important things being said. It might sound more like a voice to have it sound like someone actually said it.*

Persuasive Essay: (This writer wanted assistance in providing supporting detail in his essay). *If it were me, I might try searching for some more information that supports the formation of glaciers on the planet in the Ice Ages, just to show that global warming might be exaggerated, and for comparison and contrast. I always like to have things compared; it shocks people, and that makes it interesting.*

Fiction/Suspense: (This writer wanted help with the ending.) *It sounded like a cliff-hanger and will make the reader want to come back and read more. I might add one more hint at the end.*

Content Area Essay: (This writer wanted help with the conclusion.) *The question might be answered more directly with one more paragraph at the end explaining why it all had to end that way.*

Figure F.2 What to Look For and Respond To

6–8	9–12
• Allusion	• Alliteration
• Characterization	• Allegory
• Climax	• Antagonist
• Conflict: external, internal	• Blank verse
• Dialogue/dialect	• Characterization
• Figurative language	• Climax
• Foreshadowing	• Conflict
• Imagery	• Connotation
• Literal language	• Dynamic or round character
• Irony: situation, dramatic language	• Figurative language
• Motive	• Foreshadowing

(Continued)

Figure F.2 (Continued)

6–8	9–12
• Meaning: concrete, abstract	• Genre
• Metaphor	• Imagery
• Point of view	• Irony
• Plot	• Metaphor
• Rhyme	• Mood
• Rising action	• Narrator
• Resolution	• Personification
• Setting	• Plot
• Symbolism	• Point of view
• Theme	• Protagonist
• Tone/mood	• Stream of consciousness
	• Suspense
	• Symbolism
	• Theme
	• Tone

Other comments or notes:

_____

_____

_____

_____

Clarification questions for this draft:

_____

_____

_____

_____

8. Self-Feedback Checklist (Steps Two and Three, Writer)

Name _____

Use this checklist to determine what you as writer would like or need help with, along with what the issues are in your draft. Follow these steps:

1. Review your goals and issues or what you want help with. **Write them down below.**

2. Reread your piece silently.

3. Reread your piece aloud (it doesn't have to be in front of anyone).

4. Think about what you liked about your piece as you read it. **Jot down a few of these thoughts in the space provided.**

I liked . . .

5. Think about what you would suggest for yourself based on your goals and issues. **Write them down in the space provided.**

```
Suggestions to myself:




```

6. Now, review your notes and decide what you'll use and what you'll not use. **Write these notes in the space provided.**

```
Suggestions I will use:




```

7. Complete the **Writer Reflection Organizer**, and decide what feedback you'll keep and what you'll leave out.

8. Edit your draft using the feedback you have decided to keep.

```
Other ideas for my writing:




```

9. Editor's Before Coaching Checklist

Name _____

Directions: Use this checklist to help edit your writer's draft *before* peer coaching. Indicate in the spaces provided what the writer asked for in feedback on this piece.

Writer's Feedback (check only one):

____ Feedback on goals only ____ Feedback on issues only ____ Feedback on issues and goals

____ "I heard . . ." feedback only ____ No feedback (only available once)

Refer the writer to the Goals List, the Feedback Type Checklist, and/or the Identifying an Issue Checklist if necessary.

Writer's Issues or Goals Identified: Write down the writer's goals and issues for the draft:

_____

_____

_____

_____

_____

_____

_____

_____

_____

After looking over the above issues and goals, check them for the following (check off each when completed):

○ **Goals** set by the writer are understandable for others. Refer the writer to the Goals List for assistance and as a cross-check. **Comments for the writer:**

```
```

○ **Issues** the writer identified are understandable, and peers will know what to listen for. If an issue wasn't understandable, indicate below what the writer can do to make it easier to understand. **Comments for the writer:**

It sounds like you're struggling with . . .

I would suggest . . .

○ **Summary** suggestions for the writer: Write down important points for the writer to mention in the summary. Jot down a minimum of two to five:

```
```

10. Editor's After and Between Coaching Checklist (Steps One, Two, and Three)

This may also be used for silent peer coaching and peer coaching as questioning.

Name _____

Directions: Use this checklist to help your writers improve their pieces between peer-coaching sessions. Indicate in the spaces provided what your writer wanted for feedback on this piece.

Writer's Feedback (check only one—they can change from the first round of peer coaching):

____ Feedback on goals only ____ Feedback on issues only ____ Feedback on goals and issues

____ "I heard . . ." feedback only ____ No feedback (only available once)

You may refer the writer back to the Goals List, Feedback Type Checklist, Identifying an Issue Checklist, and/or Writer Reflection Organizer if necessary. The writer's feedback request, goals, or issues may change from the previous round—*this is OK.*

Writer's goals or issues identified: Write down anything the writer is struggling with (issues), and the goals for the draft:

Check the draft for the above issues and goals *in addition to* the following (check off each):

○ **Goals** the writer set are still reflected in the draft. **Comments for the writer:**

```
┌─────────────────────────────────────────────────────────────┐
│                                                             │
│                                                             │
│                                                             │
│                                                             │
│                                                             │
│                                                             │
│                                                             │
└─────────────────────────────────────────────────────────────┘
```

Question starters for peer coaching as questioning:

- Where is the goal in the draft?

- Is part of the goal in the draft, and if so where?

- Has the goal changed, and is this change in the draft somewhere?

Are the issues the writer identified she or he is struggling with in the writing reflected in the changes, and if so where?

Question starters:

- Where and what is the issue in this draft?

- Has the issue changed in the draft from one peer-coaching session to another?

- Was the issue resolved, and if so how, where?

- Was all helpful feedback given in previous peer-coaching sessions used in this draft?

○ **Issues** the writer identified are addressed with the writer's changes. **Comments for the writer:**

```
┌─────────────────────────────────────────────────────────────┐
│                                                             │
│                                                             │
│                                                             │
│                                                             │
│                                                             │
│                                                             │
│                                                             │
└─────────────────────────────────────────────────────────────┘
```

11. Editor's Final Checklist and Rubric (Steps One, Two, and Three)

Directions: Use this checklist to help edit your writer's piece *after all* peer-coaching sessions have finished and the paper is ready to be turned in as a final.

Writer's Feedback (check only one—they can change from the first round of peer coaching):

____ Feedback on goals only ____ Feedback on issues only ____ Feedback on goals and issues

____ "I heard . . ." feedback only ____ No feedback

You may refer the writer back to the Goals List, Feedback Type Checklist, Reflection Organizer, and/or Identifying an Issue Checklist if necessary. The writer's feedback request, goals, or issues may have changed from the previous round—*this is OK.*

Writer's Issues or Goals Identified: Write down anything the writer needed help with or the goals for the draft:

Check the draft for the above issues and goals *in addition to* the following:

○ **Goals** the writer set are still reflected in the draft. **Comments for the writer:**

```
[                                                                    ]
[                                                                    ]
[                                                                    ]
[                                                                    ]
[                                                                    ]
```

○ **Issues** the writer identified are addressed with the writer's changes. **Comments for the writer:**

```
[                                                                    ]
[                                                                    ]
[                                                                    ]
[                                                                    ]
[                                                                    ]
```

Questions for peer coaching as questioning:

Are the writing goals still reflected in the draft?

- Was feedback used that helped with the goal?
- Did the goal align with the project goal?
- Has the goal changed, and is this change in the draft somewhere?

Are the issues the writer identified, or what she or he was struggling with, reflected in the changes?

Question starters:

- What was the issue in this draft? Did additional issues arise while writing, and if so, were they addressed?
- Did all issues get resolved? If so, how? If not, why not?
- Did the issue change at all, and must it still be resolved? How can it be resolved?

Final Comments:

```
[                                                                    ]
[                                                                    ]
[                                                                    ]
[                                                                    ]
[                                                                    ]
```

Use the following rubric to evaluate all remaining areas for the writer to finalize this draft (shaded areas can be replaced with words that pertain to your assignment). Circle or highlight specific areas as needed.

	Ideas and Content	Word Choice	Conventions
5	Feedback suggestions were incorporated into the writing to make it better—ideas were clear, the topic was interesting, and information was easy to understand. All issues identified by the writer have been resolved, and the writing flows with clear understanding. All of the writing goals are met in the writing.	Word choices were appropriate and understandable, and a variety of words were used to make the reading sound intelligent and always interesting. Vocabulary taught in class was used and helped create good mind pictures and visuals. Many energetic verbs, colorful adverbs, and adjectives were used to make the writing jump out at the reader for better understanding.	This paper has very few errors, and good control of grammar as demonstrated in the following areas: • Spelling • Capitalization and punctuation • Paragraphing • Anything taken from another source is cited in the paper and on the reference page • Direct quotes are in quotation marks; longer quotes are in a separate paragraphs
3	Feedback suggestions were used in some places, but there is room for more that are not used (that can help the piece if used). Ideas were somewhat clear but could still use more detail to make them clearer. The reader will have questions that are not answered in the writing. Some or most of the writing goals were met within the writing.	Word choices were mostly appropriate, with a few areas that either seemed too hard to understand or did not have enough detail. The reading was interesting in some places and not as interesting in other places. Vocabulary taught in class was used very little or not at all. Verbs needed a little more "energy," adverbs and adjectives were used a little, with room to use more. The writing will jump out at the reader with a little more "tweaking."	A few errors in the following areas have been circled: • Spelling • Capitalization and punctuation: periods, commas, exclamation points, quotation marks, etc. • Paragraphing—new ideas have a new paragraph; new paragraphs are indented • Anything taken from another source is cited in the paper and on the reference page • Direct quotes are in quotation marks; longer quotes are in separate paragraphs
1	None of the feedback suggestions were used. Suggestions made can be worked into the piece and will improve it. Ideas were not all clear, and readers will have many questions after reading it. None or very few of the goals were met for this draft.	Word choices need to be reviewed for appropriateness. Many areas are difficult to understand. Verbs do not jump out at the reader, but with some more work on using adjectives and adverbs, they can.	Errors are in all areas indicated below: • Spelling errors • Capitalization and punctuation: periods missing, commas misplaced, exclamation points not used, quotation marks improperly placed • Paragraphing missing; new ideas were still with old ideas and was confusing to read; new paragraphs were missing indents • Information taken from other sources not cited or on the reference page • Direct quotes were not in quotation marks; longer quotes were not in separate paragraphs

12. Writer Reflection Organizer (Step Three)

Name _____

Directions: Use this form to take notes on feedback given in the peer coaching session *before* filling out the **Peer Feedback Checklist**. Write down all feedback and any immediate thoughts about it.

____ Feedback on goals only ____ Feedback on issues only ____ Feedback on goals and issues

____ "I heard . . ." feedback only ____ No feedback (only available once)

1. "I liked . . ." statements (write down the "I liked . . ." statements from your peers):

   +---+
   | |
   | |
   | |
   | |
   | |
   | |
   | |
   +---+

2. "I heard . . ." statements (write down the "I heard . . ." statements from your peers):

   +---+
   | |
   | |
   | |
   | |
   | |
   | |
   | |
   +---+

3. Suggestions for change (write down any other feedback comments and suggestions from your peers):

4. Write down your immediate thoughts on *all* feedback (things to think about):

- What feedback you *might* want to keep.

- What feedback you *know* you do not want to keep.

- What your peers liked about it, and what they liked about it the most.

- What the "I heard . . ." feedback said, and what conclusions you can draw about the "I heard . . ." statements.

- How the feedback fits in with what you asked for help with and/or what your goals are for the piece.

My thoughts . . .

13. Responder Reflection Organizer (Step Three)

Name _____

Directions: Use this form to take notes on feedback while listening in the peer-coaching session *before* filling out the **Peer Feedback Checklist**. Write down all feedback and any immediate thoughts about it afterward.

Writer feedback choice (check one):

_____ Feedback on goals only _____ Feedback on issues only _____ Feedback on goals and issues

_____ "I heard . . ." feedback only _____ No feedback (only available once)

1. Write down what you liked most about the draft (think of one to three things):

2. Write down what you heard (or read if silent peer coaching) in the writing in "I heard . . ." statements (or questions for peer coaching as questioning):

3. Suggestions for change (write down the first thoughts that come to your mind while listening):

```
┌─────────────────────────────────────────────────────────────────────┐
│                                                                       │
│                                                                       │
│                                                                       │
│                                                                       │
│                                                                       │
│                                                                       │
│                                                                       │
└─────────────────────────────────────────────────────────────────────┘
```

4. Write down your immediate thoughts on *all* feedback *during and after* reading. *Think about the following:*

- What you liked about the writing style (for example, think about the vocabulary: was it descriptive, was it organized, did every word move the main ideas along?).

- What you liked about the plot or content (for example, was it fast or slow paced? Was it informative, or was there room for more detailed information?).

- What the writer's goals were for the draft.

- What the writer wanted help with, or what the issues were in the draft.

- How the feedback given fits within the type of feedback that was asked for.

```
┌─────────────────────────────────────────────────────────────────────┐
│ Final thoughts and/or questions:                                      │
│                                                                       │
│                                                                       │
│                                                                       │
│                                                                       │
│                                                                       │
│                                                                       │
│                                                                       │
│                                                                       │
│                                                                       │
│                                                                       │
│                                                                       │
│                                                                       │
└─────────────────────────────────────────────────────────────────────┘
```

14. Writer Summary
Organizer (Step Two)

Name _____

Directions: Use this to help develop a summary of your piece for peer coaching. Write a summary of one minute (or less). You may read it from this paper, or you can say it without the paper.

1. What initially inspired you to write this, or what gave you your idea?

2. What literary genre is it (poetry, prose, essay, novel, novella, screenplay, biography, short story)?

3. What is the title of the piece?

4. What is the most important event, episode, or piece of information in this piece? Explain briefly what happens and why *without giving away any ending.*

```



```

5. Who is the main character, or who are the cast of characters?

```



```

6. Where do most of the events, or action, take place?

```



```

7. What is the second most important event or idea in this piece (this can involve a person, a place, an action, or any other information leading to something important)?

```



```

8. List any other important information you'd like to share with peers about this piece:

```



```

Now, use the information from above to write up a summary that will take no longer than one minute to tell the responders.

_____

_____

_____

_____

_____

_____

_____

_____

_____

_____

_____

_____

_____

_____

_____

_____

Congratulations! You're ready to summarize your piece for reading aloud in the peer-coaching session. You may read your summary off of this paper, or you can try to memorize it and recite it out loud.

Happy peer coaching!

15. Oral Reading Rubric (Step Two)

Name _____

Directions: Use this rubric to help the writer, or help yourself if you are the writer, read a draft aloud in a writer's voice that reflects how the piece was written or intended to sound. (Shaded areas can be replaced with more content- or assignment-specific language as needed.)

Verbal Presentation	1	2	3	4
Intonation, Pronunciation, and Elocution	**Rarely** uses a strong voice or emphasizes certain vocabulary words with passion; pronunciation is unclear, and expression **does not** convey passion. **More practice and coaching in this area strongly recommended.**	**Occasionally** uses a strong voice; emphasizes certain vocabulary words **occasionally**; uses clear pronunciation and expression that conveys passion **at times**. **More practice and coaching in this area recommended.**	**Usually** uses a strong voice; emphasizes certain vocabulary words at times; **usually** uses clear pronunciation and expression that conveys passion. **Can benefit from more practice and coaching in this area.**	Uses a strong voice with emphasis on certain vocabulary words; **always** uses clear pronunciation and expression that conveys passion.
Pitch	Does not speak loud enough; mumbles and is difficult to understand or hear. **More practice and coaching strongly recommended.**	**Occasionally** speaks loudly and clearly. Listeners can **sometimes** hear and understand. **More practice and coaching recommended.**	Speaks loudly and clearly throughout **most** of the reading. Listeners can **usually** hear and understand. **Can benefit from more practice and coaching.**	Speaks loudly and clearly throughout the **entire** reading. Listeners can always hear and understand.

Verbal Presentation	1	2	3	4
Conveyance of Author's Intended Message	The message the author is trying to convey to listeners is **neither** clear nor understandable. **More practice and coaching on summarization strongly recommended.**	It is **difficult** to understand the message the author is trying to convey to listeners. **More practice and coaching on summarization recommended.**	It is **somewhat easy** and clear to understand the message the author is trying to convey to listeners. **Can use more practice and coaching on summarization.**	It is **easy** to understand what the author is trying to convey to listeners.

Nonverbal Presentation	1	2	3	4
Posture, Poise, and Eye Contact	**Rarely** makes direct eye contact with listeners; looks at notes 100% of the time; holds paper in front of face; seems to lack confidence when reading. **Needs more practice and coaching in this area.**	**Occasionally** uses direct eye contact; looks at notes most of the time; stands up straight for the most part, usually holds paper below neck; **doesn't** seem confident or relaxed. **Needs more practice and coaching in this area.**	**Sometimes** uses direct eye contact; looks at notes at times; stands up straight, holds paper below neck; seems pretty much confident and **almost** relaxed. **Can use more practice and coaching in this area.**	**Always** uses direct eye contact, rarely looking at notes; stands up straight; holds paper below neck; seems confident and relaxed.
Audience/ Listener Persuasion	**Unsuccessful** in persuading the listeners of a position or **does not** hold their attention **at all**. **More practice and coaching in this area strongly recommended.**	**Slightly successful** in persuading the listeners of a position; holds listeners' attention for only a short period of time. **Needs more practice and coaching in this area.**	Is **somewhat successful** in persuading the listeners of a position, holding their attention **at times. Can use more practice and coaching in this area.**	Does an **excellent** job of persuading the listeners of a position, consistently holding their attention.

Total Oral Reading Score: _____ /20

    16–20: Outstanding!

    11–15: Good and getting better.

    6–10: Room for improvement—keep practicing.

    5: Needs much more practice (see below).

Additional Comments:

16. Good Listening Rubric

Directions: Use this rubric to help you listen effectively and actively when the writer reads his or her piece aloud. Use it as a guide to improve on your listening the next time. Refer to the **Active Listening Checklist** for reminders about good, effective listening.

Listening and Responding	*1*	*2*	*3*	*4*
Attention on the Speaker	Did not face body toward, or look at, the speaker. Did not take notes; talked while the writer was reading.	*Occasionally* faced the speaker; looked at the speaker 50% to 65% of the time. Took very few notes; spoke to others at times while the writer was reading.	*Usually* had body positioned toward speaker, looking away occasionally. Took some notes and did not speak while the reader read.	Positioned body toward speaker, or looked at speaker, 95% to 100% of the time. Only looked away to take notes. Did not talk at all.
Recording Information and Making Mental Summaries	Took *no* notes while the writer read or immediately after. Made *no* mental notes during the reading to help remember.	Took *very few* notes while the writer read or immediately after. *Very few* notes focused on feedback on goals, issues, and feedback request. Made *very few* mental notes during the reading, sometimes by paying attention to body language to help remember.	Took *some* notes while the writer read or immediately after. *Some* of the notes focused on feedback on goals, issues, and feedback request. Made *a few* mental notes during the reading, sometimes by paying attention to body language to help remember.	Took notes during or immediately after the reading by recording thoughts related to feedback request, writer goals, and issues. Made *several* mental notes during reading by paying attention to speaker's body language to help remember important information.

Listening and Responding	1	2	3	4
Avoiding Distractions	Gave in to *numerous* outside distractions; gave *very little* (if any) attention to the writer while reading.	Gave *much more* than 30% to other thoughts; gave outside distractions *much* attention.	Gave *slightly more* than 30% to other thoughts; gave outside distractions *a little* attention.	Gave no more than 30% to other thoughts; did not give distractions any attention.
Listening With Intention: Body Language	Did *not* sit facing the reader; hands were *not* on desk and were fidgeting with other things or were not visible.	Sat *somewhat* upright, did *not* face the reader; hands were *not* on desk where they could be seen.	Sat *somewhat* upright, *mostly* facing the reader with hands on desk where they could be seen.	Sat upright with hands on desk, *directly* facing the reader, pen or pencil in hand to take notes.
Listening With Intention: Asking Clarification Questions	*Did not* ask writer questions to clarify understanding on goals, issues, or anything read in the draft.	Asked writer one question to clarify understanding on goals, issues, or something read in the draft.	Asked writer *a few* questions to clarify understanding on goals, issues, or something read in the draft.	Asked writer questions to clarify understanding on goals, issues, or something read in the draft.
Reflection and Follow-up	*Did not* use the Responder Reflection Organizer to take notes on during or after the reading. *Did not* reflect on the writer's goals, issues, or feedback request.	Did *not use*, or used *very little*, the Responder Reflection Organizer to take notes on during or after the reading. *Did not* review or reflect on any notes after the reading.	*Sometimes* used Responder Reflection Organizer to take a few notes on during or after the reading. Reflected on the writer's goals, issues, and feedback request by looking *briefly* at notes after reading.	Used the Responder Reflection Organizer to take notes on during or after the reading. Reflected on the writer's goals, issues, and feedback request by looking *thoroughly* at notes after reading.

6 7 8 9 10 11 12 13 14 15 16 17 18 19 20 21 22 23 24

Practice needed   Getting better   Good to excellent listening skills!

17. Manager's Checklist

Name _____

Directions: Use this to help your peer-coaching buddies make sure they follow all the steps. Check off the areas as they apply.

WRITER

Setting goals:

____ Filled out the Goals Sheet to set goals

____ Communicated goals to your peer or peers

Identified a trouble spot or issue:

____ Used the Feedback Type Checklist

Wrote or prepared a summary to read:

____ Used Summary Organizer

Reflected on feedback to determine what to use and what to leave out:

____ Used Writer Reflection Organizer *or*

____ Took notes on the suggestions offered

RESPONDER

Used "I liked" and "I heard . . ." statements when giving feedback:

____ Used the Peer Feedback Checklist

____ Responded to what the writer asked for

____ Asked clarification questions when necessary

____ Did not use the word *you* other than in a question or "I liked . . ." statement.

> **Comments:**

> **Comments:**

EDITOR

Checked writer's draft before first peer-coaching session:

_____ Used Editor's Checklist Before Coaching

Checked writer's draft after first peer-coaching session:

_____ Used Editor's Checklist After and
Between Coaching

Checked writer's draft after final peer-coaching session:

_____ Used Editor's Final Checklist and
Rubric

Comments:

Good work, Coach!

18. Teacher Anecdotal Notes Record for Writers (Steps One, Two, and Three)

Use this to record student behavioral information when circulating among peer-coaching sessions while students work in groups or buddy sessions.

Class/Group: _____ Student: _____ Date: _____

Goal Setting:

_____ Understanding of goal setting is evidenced by goals that are focused and achievable.

_____ Uses available tools for assistance when needed.

_____ Goals align with assignment expectations or project goals.

_____ Goals align with learning standards or identified benchmarks.

Comments:

Feedback Requests:

_____ Uses goals as catalyst or springboard for establishing feedback.

_____ Identifies issues that focus on improving the draft.

_____ Articulates competence and confidence when communicating issues or struggles within writing to peers.

_____ Demonstrates a willingness to receive feedback and improve the draft.

_____ Uses analysis, as demonstrated through the Identifying an Issue Checklist, to determine issues in writing.

Comments:

Summary:

_____ Prepared a summary ahead of time, using highlighted information.

_____ Used Summary Organizer as needed.

_____ Read or recited summary in one minute or less.

_____ Recited summary without reading.

_____ Articulated most crucial information, or main points, with understanding.

Comments:

Oral Recitation:

_____ Read or recited with intonation and expression.

_____ Used eye contact occasionally while reading.

Comments:

Feedback and Reflection:

_____ Called on one person at a time.

_____ Took notes or used Reflection Organizer to record feedback.

_____ Applied a think-through process to determine what feedback to use and what to leave out; applied reflection using the Reflection Organizer.

_____ Reconciled feedback with goals and issues stated while developing an understanding of the analytical thinking needed to arrive at feedback decisions.

_____ Sought assistance from editor as needed.

Comments:

19. Teacher Anecdotal Notes Record for Responders (Steps One, Two, and Three)

Use this to record student behavioral information when circulating among peer coaching sessions while students work in groups or buddy sessions.

Class/Group: _____ Student: _____ Date: _____

Listening:

_____ Took notes on what the writer wanted for feedback and/or used Peer Feedback Checklist and Responder Reflection Organizer.

_____ Recorded thoughts while writer was reading and reflected on these notes prior to giving feedback.

_____ Demonstrated active listening behaviors, such as not speaking while writer was reading, seemed attentive, looked at the reader, wrote down thoughts as they came; exhibited attributes from the Active Listening Checklist.

_____ Feedback/suggestions offered focused exclusively on what the writer stated she or he needed help with.

_____ Feedback/suggestions went *beyond* what the writer stated she or he needed help with.

_____ Feedback/suggestions aligned with writer's stated goal for the draft.

Comments:

Responding:

_____ Responded appropriately to the feedback request in general.

_____ Responded with "I like . . ." and at least one "I heard . . ." statement before making any suggestions.

_____ Used appropriate prompts, as suggested on Peer Feedback Checklist, when responding with suggestions.

_____ Avoided the use of "you" statements, unless in a question or within the "I liked . . ." response or a question.

_____ Responses were appropriate to the genre of the draft.

Comments:

Other Comments or Concerns:

20. Teacher Anecdotal Notes Record for Editors (Steps One, Two, and Three)

Use this to record student behavioral information when circulating among peer-coaching sessions while students work in groups or buddy sessions.

Class/Group: _____ Student: _____ Date: _____

Feedback Review:

_____ Checked the writing for goals alignment as identified in the Goals List.

_____ Checked the writer's draft for suggestions using the Responder Reflection Organizer.

_____ Feedback/suggestions used applied exclusively to what the writer asked for help in, and helped the writer import feedback into the writing.

_____ Feedback/suggestions aligned with writer's stated goals for the draft.

Comments:

Summary Review:

_____ Helped the writer prepare a summary to read for peer-coaching session.

_____ Responded with "I like . . ." statements before making any suggestions when helping.

_____ Offered assistance as needed in using the Summary Organizer and in highlighting information to prepare for the summary.

_____ Helpful suggestions were appropriate to the draft and formation of a summary.

Comments:

Ideas/Content/Word Choice/Conventions:

_____ Checked and gave helpful suggestions for grammar, usage, and writing conventions using rubric in Editor's Final Checklist.

_____ Checked and gave helpful suggestions for overall ideas and content for organization and clarity using rubric in Editor's Final Checklist.

_____ Checked and gave feedback on word choice for syntax, semantics, writing flow, clarity, and articulation using rubric in Editor's Final Checklist, using "I liked . . ." statements first.

_____ Checked and gave feedback, using "I liked . . ." statements first, on overall writing flow.

Comments:

21. Teacher Anecdotal Notes Record for Managers (Steps One, Two, and Three)

Use this to record student behavioral information when circulating among peer-coaching sessions while students work in groups or buddy sessions.

Class/Group: _____ Student: _____ Date: _____

Manager as Session Organizer:

_____ Class or group peer coaching: checked to be sure all had a chance to be writer.

_____ Class, group, or buddy peer coaching: checked to be sure each writer had an editor at some point.

_____ Buddy peer coaching: made sure that each had a turn to be writer and responder.

_____ Checked to be sure each role had its corresponding checklist or organizer; offered assistance when they did not.

_____ Made sure that each writer was prepared with a summary.

_____ Made sure each writer had goals and issues established.

_____ Made sure each writer was prepared with a feedback option selected.

Comments/Suggestions for Future Sessions:

Manager as Role Checker:

_____ Checked to be sure each student remained with, and followed through on, assigned role.

_____ Offered assistance to anyone confused on or in need of help in the fulfillment of his or her role.

_____ Understood the function of each role and its corresponding rubric, checklist, and organizer.

_____ Circulated the area assigned to him or her: class, group, or buddy sessions.

_____ Used the Manager's Checklist for assistance in following through on responsibilities of managers and helping others fulfill their roles effectively.

Comments:

Manager as Learner:

_____ Gleaned helpful information about the student peer-coaching process through observation and evaluation of others as they fulfilled their roles.

_____ Achieved a deeper, clearer understanding of each of the roles and steps within the roles.

_____ Developed a better sense of competence and confidence about fulfilling and mastering steps and protocols in the student peer-coaching process.

Comments:

22. Peer Role Evaluation Rubric for Writer

Directions: This rubric will help you coach and evaluate your peers as they fulfill the role of writer, helping them become *better* writers, communicators, speakers, and readers. Use this rubric to rate and give feedback about progress in setting goals, asking for feedback, summarizing, reading aloud, and using the feedback from peers to revise writing drafts. (Shaded areas can be replaced with words that pertain specifically to the assignment.)

Steps One and Two: goal setting, setting feedback, summarizing

Goal setting *Goals List* *(No. 1)*	Unfocused goals; difficult to tell if they can be achieved or not. Assistance is needed in matching up with project/task objectives set by the teacher. *Not clear* or understandable to peer coaching group/buddy. 1–2 ____	Goals are *somewhat* focused, not sure if they can be achieved, and can probably use some assistance in matching up with project/task objectives; clear and understandable to peer coaching group/buddy. 3–4 ____	Goals are focused, achievable, and match up with project/task objectives set by the teacher; clear and understandable to peer coaching group/buddy. 5–6 ____
Feedback setting *Feedback Type Checklist (No. 5)*	Genre and subject either not identified or identified *with lots of assistance*; communication to peers was not clear; issues either were not communicated or lacked enough detail to make sense; "I" statements were *not* used to communicate an issue; feedback option was either *not* communicated to peers or communicated with very little detail (peers had questions). 1–2 ____	Genre and subject identified *with assistance* and communicated to peers (peers had some questions); issues communicated lacked detail; "I" statements may have been used to communicate an issue; feedback option communicated to peers with *little* detail (peers may have had questions). 3–4 ____	Genre and subject identified and communicated *clearly* to peers; issues communicated clearly and with detail; "I" statements were used to communicate an issue; feedback option clearly communicated to peers with detail. 5–6 ____

Summarizing *Writer Summary Organizer* *(No. 14)*	Summary was *not clearly* focused or communicated effectively to peers (or was not communicated at all). Peers were not sure what it was about. 1–2 ____	Summary was *somewhat* focused with *enough* detail; *some* important ideas/information from the Summary Organizer was communicated to peers, though unclear what it was about. 3–4 ____	Summary stated was focused and to the point with *all or most* areas on the Summary Organizer communicated clearly to peers leaving no questions as to what the piece was about. 5–6 ____
Reading Aloud *Oral Reading Rubric (No. 15)* Circle here if piece was read by another peer.	Selected piece was *not* read with expression, intonation, or passion, and more coaching is needed here. 1–2 ____	Selected piece was read with expression, intonation, and passion. 3–4 ____	Selected piece was read with *outstanding* expression, intonation, and passion. 5–6 ____

Step Three: reflecting, decision making, editing

Reflection *Responder Reflection Organizer (No. 13)*	Notes were *not* taken while feedback was given. No reflection on feedback was noted. 1–2 ____	*Some* notes were taken while feedback was given using Responder Reflection Organizer or a journal; some or little discussion with peers on feedback, either through questions or in buddy discussion. 3–4 ____	Notes were taken while feedback was given using Reflection Organizer or a journal; discussion with peers or buddy immediately followed. Some questions were asked for clarification and deeper reflection. 5–6 ____
Use of Feedback *Writer Reflection Organizer (No. 12)*	Writer *did not* review goals and issues stated to peers for comparing feedback; writing style was *not* a consideration; either no feedback was used, or what was used was not important to the revision process, stated issues, and goals of the draft. 1–2 ____	Writer *may have* reviewed goals and issues stated to peers to compare with feedback; writing style was given *little or no* consideration; feedback taken was *somewhat* important to the revision process, stated issues, and goals of the draft. 3–4 ____	Writer reviewed goals and issues stated to peers to compare with feedback; consideration was given to writing style; feedback taken was important to the revision process, stated issues, and goals of the draft. 5–6 ____

Use of Editor ○ Check here if editor was NOT used	Editorial assistance was offered but not used. No suggestions were taken for revision. 1–2 ____	Editorial assistance was offered, though suggestions were not used at all, or they were only partially included in any revisions. 3–4 ____	Editorial assistance was sought and used. Revisions were made according to suggestions. 5–6 ____
Revision Process	*No* revisions were made, and writing *was not* prepared for more peer coaching or final copy. 1–2 ____	*Some* revisions were made, and writing *was* prepared for more peer coaching or final copy. 3–4 ____	*All* necessary revisions were made, and writing *was* prepared for more peer coaching or final copy. 5–6 ____

Comments/Suggestions:

Total Peer Coaching Writer Score ____ /48

8–16: Needs more coaching

17–23: Making progress!

24–31: Getting better!

32–39: Almost there . . .

40–48: Expert!

23. Peer Role Evaluation Rubric for Responder

Directions: This rubric will help you coach and evaluate your peers as they fulfill the role of responder. Use this rubric to rate and give feedback about their progress in giving the writer feedback on goals and issues. (Shaded areas can be replaced with words that pertain specifically to the assignment.)

Steps One and Two: Listening

Listening for the Writer's Feedback Request *Peer Feedback Checklist (No. 7)* *Responder Reflection Organizer (No. 13)*	Responder took *no* notes and wrote *no* issues, goals, and feedback request *on Peer Feedback Checklist* or anywhere else in response to what the writer asked for. 1–2 ____	Responder took *a few* notes, wrote an issue, goals, and feedback request *on Peer Feedback Checklist* or somewhere else in response to what the writer asked for. 3–4 ____	Responder took *thorough* notes and recorded writer's issues, goals, and feedback request *on Peer Feedback Checklist* or somewhere else in response to what the writer asked for. 5–6 ____
Listening for the Writer's Goals Statement *Active Listening Checklist (No. 6)*	*No* or *few* listening points on the *Active Listening Checklist* were followed. 1–2 ____	*Some* listening points on the *Active Listening Checklist* were followed. 3–4 ____	All listening points on the *Active Listening Checklist* were followed. 5–6 ____

Step Three: Responding/giving feedback

Reflection on Feedback *Responder Reflection Organizer (No. 13)*	Responder *did not* take notes or write thoughts while writer read. 1–2 ____	Responder *took a few* notes and/or wrote thoughts while writer read; notes focused on writer issue, goals, and feedback request. 3–4 ____	Responder took thorough notes and/or wrote thoughts while writer read; notes/thoughts focused on writer issues, goals, and feedback request. If no notes were taken, all responses were focused on feedback writer asked for. 5–6 ____
Focus on Feedback *Peer Feedback Checklist (No. 7)*	Did not focus any feedback on what the writer asked for or stated as a goal, or in response to feedback option. 1–2 ____	Focused *somewhat* on writer's stated goals, issues, and feedback request. Used checklist to help focus. 3–4 ____	Focused *precisely and accurately* on writer's stated goals, issues, and feedback request. May have used checklist to help focus. 5–6 ____
Giving Feedback *Peer Feedback Checklist (No. 7)*	"I liked . . ." statements were *rarely* or *not at all* used; "I heard . . ." was *not* responded to when asked for; suggestions were not helpful. 1–2 ____	"I liked . . ." statement *sometimes* used first; "I heard . . ." used *at times* when asked for. Suggestions were helpful and *somewhat* focused. 3–4 ____	"I liked . . ." statement used first, followed by "I heard . . ."; more given when asked for. Suggestions were very helpful and highly focused on writer's goals and issues. 5–6 ____
Overall Use of Peer-Coaching Protocol for Responder	Needs more assistance in being a responder in peer coaching. 1–2 ____	OK. At times responsive, somewhat helpful. 3–4 ____	Excellent. Responsive, focused, highly helpful. 5–6 ____

Total Peer Coaching Responder Score: ____ /36

6–12: Needs more coaching

13–18: Making progress!

19–23: Getting better!

24–29: Almost there . . .

30–36: Expert!

24. Peer Role Evaluation Rubric for Editor

Directions: This rubric will help you coach and evaluate your peers as they fulfill the role of editor, helping them become *better* at reviewing and editing. (Shaded areas can be replaced with words that pertain specifically to the assignment.)

Steps One, Two, and Three

Goal-Setting Checks *Editor's Before Coaching Checklist (No. 9)* *Editor's After and Between Coaching Checklist (No. 10)*	*Did not* take notes or indicate writer goals on checklist; did not check goals against project/ task goals set by teacher. 1–2 ____	*May have* indicated or taken *some* notes on checklist of writer goals; checked that *some* goals matched project/task goals set by teacher. 3–4 ____	Indicated or took notes on checklist of writer's goals; checked that *all* goals matched project/ task goals set by teacher. 5–6 ____
Feedback/ Issues Checks *Editor's Before Coaching Checklist (No. 9)* *Editor's After and Between Coaching Checklist (No. 10)*	*Briefly* checked writer's issue for clarity; made few or no suggestions for help in preparing the writer's writing for peer coaching. 1–2 ____	*Reviewed* writer's issue for understanding by peers for their feedback; gave assistance on other areas when asked; made some suggestions for help in preparing the writer's writing for peer coaching. 3–4 ____	Thoroughly checked writer's issues for understanding by peers for their feedback; offered thorough assistance and made suggestions to help the writer prepare for peer coaching. 5–6 ____

Summarizing Checks *Editor's Before Coaching Checklist (No. 9)* *Editor's After and Between Coaching Checklist (No. 10)*	Made *few* or no helpful suggestions to the writer to help prepare summary for peer coaching. *Did not* review or refer writer to Summary Organizer. 1–2 ____	Made *some* helpful suggestions to the writer as needed to help prepare summary for peer coaching. *Briefly* reviewed Summary Organizer. 3–4 ____	Made *many* helpful suggestions as needed to the writer to help prepare summary for peer coaching. Reviewed and referred writer to Summary Organizer. 5–6 ____

Step Three: Writer final review and feedback

Goal-Setting Checks *Editor's Final Checklist (No. 11)*	*Little or no* attempt to review or check final writer goals. Most or all effort was initiated by writer. 1–2 ____	Referred the writer to *some* goals to make sure they were in the final draft. 3–4 ____	Kept track of *all* writer's goals to make sure they were met in the final draft; reviewed all writer Goals Lists. 5–6 ____
Evaluation of Writer *Editor's Final Checklist (No. 11)*	*No* final checks or suggestions for the writer were offered. Rubric on Editor's Final Checklist was not applied to the final draft. 1–2 ____	Checked the writer's final piece and offered *a few* suggestions as needed. Used rubric on Editor's Final Checklist to help writer *without* reviewing it together. 3–4 ____	Thoroughly checked the writer's final piece and *offered suggestions* as needed. Used rubric on Editor's Final Checklist to help writer on final piece, and reviewed it thoroughly with writer. 5–6 ____
Comments/Suggestions:			

Total Peer Coaching Editor Score: ____ /30

5–10: Needs more coaching

11–15: Making progress!

16–20: Getting better!

21–25: Almost there . . .

26–30: Expert!

25. Peer Role Evaluation Rubric for Manager

Directions: This rubric will help you coach and evaluate your peers as they fulfill the role of manager. This evaluation will help them become *better* organizers, role checkers, and managers, which will help everyone be better at peer coaching. Use this rubric to rate and give feedback about how the manager is doing in each area listed and described below.

Steps One, Two, and Three: Organization and role checking

Writer Checks *Manager's Checklist (No. 17)*	*Did not* offer assistance or use the Manager's Checklist to help the writer. 1–2 ____	Offered *some* assistance in fulfilling the writer role, though did not necessarily use the Manager's Checklist. 3–4 ____	*Used* the Manager's Checklist to assist and help writer fulfill his or her role. 5–6 ____
Responder Checks *Manager's Checklist (No. 17)*	*Did not* offer assistance or use the Manager's Checklist to help the responder. 1–2 ____	Offered *some* assistance in fulfilling the responder role, though did not necessarily use the Manager's Checklist. 3–4 ____	*Used* the Manager's Checklist to assist and help responder fulfill his or her role. 5–6 ____
Editor Checks *Manager's Checklist (No. 17)*	*Did not* offer assistance or use the Manager's Checklist to help the editor. 1–2 ____	Offered *some* assistance in fulfilling the editor role, though did not necessarily use the Manager's Checklist. 3–4 ____	*Used* the Manager's Checklist to assist and help editor fulfill his or her role. 5–6 ____

Teacher's Helper/Organizer Manager's Checklist (No. 17)	*Slightly* helpful in organizing and setting up peer coaching; did not initiate help, rather was reminded or told by teacher how to organize, arrange chairs, etc. 1–2 ____	*Somewhat* helpful in organizing peer-coaching sessions by helping the teacher with roles, arranging chairs, checking on roles, handing out materials, etc. 3–4 ____	Organized and set up peer-coaching sessions by *helping* the teacher with roles, arranging chairs, checking on roles, handing out materials, etc. 5–6 ____

Total Peer Coaching Manager Score: ____ /24

4–8: Needs more coaching

9–12: Making progress!

13–16: Getting better!

17–20: Almost there . . .

21–24: Expert!

26. Teacher Role Evaluation Rubric for Writer

Directions: Use this rubric to evaluate students as they fulfill the writer role in the following areas: goal setting, identifying issues in writing, making and articulating feedback choices, summarizing, oral reading, reflection on feedback, and overall application of the peer coaching protocols. (Shaded areas can be replaced with content-specific language.)

Steps One and Two: goal setting, setting feedback, summarizing, oral reading

Goal Setting *Goals List (No. 1)*	Unfocused goals; difficult to gauge achievement; required much assistance in aligning student-set goals to project/task objectives. Lack of verbal/oral articulation in peer-coaching peers. 1–2 _____	Goals are somewhat focused, though may lack achievability; assistance required in aligning student-set goals to project/task objectives; clear and understandable to peer-coaching peers. 3–4 _____	Goals are focused and achievable, and align with project/task objectives set by the teacher; articulated clearly and understandably to peer-coaching peers. 5–6 _____
Feedback Setting *Identifying an Issue Checklist (No. 4)* *Feedback Type Checklist (No. 5)*	Genre and subject not identified or identified with assistance; communication lacked articulation; issues either not communicated or lacked enough detail to make sense; feedback option lacked clarity, articulation, and detail; feedback option did not align with goals and/or issues (peers had questions). 1–2 _____	Genre and subject identified and communicated to peers with slight confusion (peers had questions); issues lacked detail and articulation; feedback option communicated with some clarity, articulation, and detail; feedback option adequately aligned with goals and/or issues (peers may have had questions). 3–4 _____	Genre and subject identified and articulated clearly to peers; issues communicated clearly and with detail; feedback option communicated with clarity and detail; feedback option in alignment with goals and/or issues. 5–6 _____

Summarizing *Summary Organizer* *(No. 14)*	Summary was not clearly focused or communicated with articulation, or was not communicated at all. Summary Organizer was missing information, or not filled out at all. Peers had many questions and confusion lingered. 1–2 ____	Summary was somewhat focused, contained *enough* detail with articulation; most areas on Summary Organizer were completed, though not all information was communicated; peers had some confusion and/or questions. 3–4 ____	Summary was focused and to the point with *all or most* areas on Summary Organizer communicated with articulation and complete clarity. Peers had very few, if any, questions. 5–6 ____
Oral Reading *Oral Reading Rubric (No. 15)*	Selected piece was *not* read with expression, intonation, or passion. More coaching is recommended. 1–2 ____	Selected piece was read with some expression, intonation, and passion. 3–4 ____	Selected piece was read with expression, intonation, and passion. 5–6 ____

Steps Two and Three: Reflecting, decision-making, editing

Reflection *Writer Reflection Organizer (No. 12)*	Notes were *not* taken while feedback was given. No reflection on feedback was noted. 1–2 ____	*Some* notes were taken while feedback was given using Reflection Organizer or a journal; some or little discussion with peers on feedback. 3–4 ____	Notes were taken while feedback was given using Reflection Organizer or a journal; discussion with peers or buddy. Some questions were asked. 5–6 ____
Use of Feedback *Writer Reflection Organizer (No. 12)*	Writer *did not* review goals and issues stated to peers for comparing feedback; writing style was *not* a consideration; either no feedback was used, or what was used was not important to the revision process, stated issues, and goals of the draft. 1–2 ____	Writer *may have* reviewed goals and issues stated to peers to compare with feedback; writing style was given *little or no* consideration; feedback taken was *somewhat* important to the revision process, stated issues, and goals of the draft. 3–4 ____	Writer reviewed goals and issues stated to peers to compare with feedback; consideration was given to writing style; feedback taken was important to the revision process, stated issues, and goals of the draft. 5–6 ____

Use of Editor ○ Check here if editor was NOT used	Editorial assistance was offered but not used. No suggestions were taken for revision. 1–2 ____	Editorial assistance was offered, though suggestions were not used at all or only partially included in any revisions. 3–4 ____	Editorial assistance was sought and used. Revisions were made according to suggestions. 5–6 ____
Revision Process	*No* revisions were made and writing was not prepared for more peer coaching or final copy. 1–2 ____	*Some* revisions were made and writing was prepared for more peer coaching or final copy. 3–4 ____	*All* necessary revisions were made and writing was prepared for more peer coaching or final copy. 5–6 ____

Total Score: ____ /48

Assistance or reteaching	*Transitioning*	Good progress	*Transitioning*	Excellent progress!
8 9 10 11 12 13 14 15 16	*17 18 19 20 21 22 23*	24 25 26 27 28 29 30	*31 32 33 34 35 36 37 38 39*	40 41 42 43 44 45 46 47 48

27. Teacher Role Evaluation Rubric for Responder

Directions: Use this rubric to evaluate students as they fulfill the responder role in the following areas: active listening, reflecting on feedback, articulating targeted feedback, use of spoken protocols, and overall application of the peer coaching protocols. (Shaded areas can be replaced with content-specific language.)

Steps One and Two: Active listening, responding

Listening for the Writer's Feedback Request *Peer Feedback Checklist (No. 7)* *Responder Reflection Organizer (No. 13)*	*No* notes taken on issues, goals, and feedback request *on Peer Feedback Checklist* or anywhere else. 1–2 ____	Responder took *a few* notes and wrote on issues, goals, and feedback request *on Peer Feedback Checklist* in response to the writer's request for feedback. 3–4 ____	Responder took *thorough* notes and wrote issues, goals, and feedback request stated by the writer *on Peer Feedback Checklist.* 5–6 ____
Listening for the Writer's Goals Statement *Active Listening Checklist (No. 6)*	*No* or *few* listening points on the *Active Listening Checklist* were adhered to. 1–2 ____	*Some* listening points on the *Active Listening Checklist* were adhered to. 3–4 ____	All listening points on the *Active Listening Checklist* were adhered to. 5–6 ____

Step Three: Responding/giving feedback

Reflection on Feedback *Responder Reflection Organizer (No. 13)*	Responder *did not* take notes and/or write thoughts while writer read. 1–2 ____	Responder *took a few* notes and/or wrote thoughts while writer read; notes focused on writer issues, goals, and feedback request. 3–4 ____	Responder took notes and/or wrote thoughts while writer read; notes/thoughts focused on writer's issues, goals, and feedback request. 5–6 ____

Focus on Feedback *Peer Feedback Checklist (No. 7)*	Did not focus any feedback on what the writer asked for, stated as a goal, or in response to feedback option. 1–2 ____	Focused *somewhat* on writer's stated goals, issues, or feedback request. Used checklist to help focus. 3–4 ____	Focused precisely and accurately on writer's stated goals, issues, and feedback request. May have used checklist to help focus. 5–6 ____
Giving Feedback *Peer Feedback Checklist (No. 7)*	"I liked . . ." statements were *rarely* or *not at all* used; "I heard . . ." was *not* responded to when asked for; suggestions were not helpful. 1–2 ____	"I liked . . ." statement *sometimes* used first; "I heard . . ." *at times* when asked for. Suggestions were helpful and *somewhat* focused. 3–4 ____	"I liked . . ." statement used first; followed with "I heard . . ." when asked for. Suggestions were very helpful and highly focused. 5–6 ____
Overall Use of Peer-Coaching Protocol for Responder	Additional assistance needed in fulfilling responder role. 1–2 ____	Adequate. At times responsive, somewhat helpful. 3–4 ____	Excellent. Responsive, focused, highly helpful. 5–6 ____

Total Score: ____ /36

Assistance or reteaching	*Transitioning*	Good progress	*Transitioning*	Excellent progress!
6 7 8 9 10 11 12	*13 14 15 16 17 18*	19 20 21 22 23	*24 25 26 27 28 29*	30 31 32 33 34 35 36

28. Teacher Role Evaluation Rubric for Editor

Directions: Use this rubric to evaluate students as they fulfill the editor role in editing, peer review, peer-coaching protocol checks, feedback checks, summarizing, and goal setting. (Shaded areas can be replaced with content-specific language.)

Steps One and Two: Writer review, feedback before, during, and after coaching sessions

Goal-Setting Checks *Editor's Before Coaching Checklist (No. 9)* *Editor's After and Between Coaching Checklist (No. 10)*	Did not take notes or indicate writer's goals on Editor's Checklists; did not align goals with project/task objectives. 1–2 ____	*May have* indicated or taken *some* notes on Editor's Checklists; aligned *some* goals with project/task goals set by teacher. 3–4 ____	Indicated or took notes on Editor's Checklists; checked that *all* goals aligned with project/task goals as set by teacher. 5–6 ____
Feedback/ Issues Checks *Editor's Before Coaching Checklist (No. 9)* *Editor's After and Between Coaching Checklist (No. 10)*	Briefly checked writer's issue for clarity; made few or no suggestions for help in preparing the writer's writing for peer coaching. 1–2 ____	Glossed over writer's issues for understanding by peers; offered assistance when asked; made some suggestions to writer for preparing writing for peer coaching. 3–4 ____	Thoroughly checked writer's issues for understanding by peers; initiated and offered thorough assistance; made suggestions to writer in preparation for peer coaching. 5–6 ____
Summarizing Checks *Editor's Before Coaching Checklist (No. 9)* *Editor's After and Between Coaching Checklist (No. 10)*	Made few or no helpful suggestions to the writer to help in preparing summary for peer coaching. 1–2 ____	Made some helpful suggestions to the writer as needed in preparing summary for peer coaching. 3–4 ____	Made many helpful suggestions as needed to the writer in preparing summary for peer coaching. 5–6 ____

Step Three: Writer final review and feedback

Goal-Setting Checks *Editor's Final Checklist* *(No. 11)*	Little or no attempt to review or check final writer's goals. Most or all effort was initiated by writer. 1–2 ____	Referred the writer to *some* goals to make sure they were in the final draft. Some initiation by writer, some by editor. 3–4 ____	Kept track of *all* writer's goals to ensure they were reflected in the final draft; reviewed all writer's Goals Lists. 5–6 ____
Writing Review and Incorporation of Feedback *Editor's Final Checklist* *(No. 11)*	No final checks or suggestions for the writer were offered. Rubric on Editor's Final Checklist was not applied to the final draft. 1–2 ____	Checked the writer's final piece and offered a few suggestions as needed. Used rubric on Editor's Final Checklist to help writer *without* reviewing it together. 3–4 ____	Thoroughly checked the writer's final piece and offered suggestions as needed. Used rubric on Editor's Final Checklist to help writer on final piece, reviewing thoroughly with writer. 5–6 ____
Comments/Suggestions:			

Total Score: ____ /30

Assistance or reteaching	*Transitioning*	Adequate progress	*Transitioning*	Excellent progress!
5 6 7 8 9 10	*11 12 13 14*	15 16 17 18 19	*20 21 22 23 24*	25 26 27 28 29 30

29. Teacher Role Evaluation Rubric for Manager

Directions: This rubric is designed to evaluate students as they fulfill the manager's role. Use it to provide managers with feedback on their application of organizational assistance for peer coaching sessions, checks on peers as they execute their roles in the peer coaching process, and their role overall as a coach for the coaches.

Step One: Organization and role checking

Writer Checks *Manager's Checklist (No. 17)*	Did not offer assistance or use the Manager's Checklist to help the writer. 1–2 ____	Offered *some* assistance in fulfilling the writer role, though did not necessarily use the Manager's Checklist. 3–4 ____	Used the Manager's Checklist to assist and support writer's fulfilling his or her role. 5–6 ____
Responder Checks *Manager's Checklist (No. 17)*	Did not offer assistance or use the Manager's Checklist to help the responder. 1–2 ____	Offered *some* assistance in fulfilling the responder role, though did not necessarily use the Manager's Checklist. 3–4 ____	Used the Manager's Checklist to assist and support responder fulfilling his or her role. 5–6 ____
Editor Checks *Manager's Checklist (No. 17)*	Did not offer assistance or use the Manager's Checklist to help the editor. 1–2 ____	Offered *some* assistance in fulfilling the editor role, though did not necessarily use the Manager's Checklist. 3–4 ____	Used the Manager's Checklist to assist and support editor's fulfilling his or her role. 5–6 ____

Teacher's Helper/ Organizer *Manager's Checklist (No. 17)*	Slightly helpful in organizing and setting up peer coaching; did not initiate help; was reminded or told by teacher how and where to organize, arranging chairs, etc. 1–2 ____	Somewhat helpful in organizing and setting up peer-coaching sessions; helped organize roles, arranging chairs, checking on roles, handing out materials, etc. 3–4 ____	Very helpful in organizing and setting up peer-coaching sessions by helping organize roles, arranging chairs, checking on roles, handing out materials, etc. 5–6 ____

Total Score: ____ /24

Needs assistance or reteaching	*Transitioning*	Adequate progress	*Transitioning*	Excellent progress!
4 5 6 7 8	*9 10 11 12*	13 14 15 16	*17 18 19*	20 21 22 23 24

Comments/Suggestions:

30. Role Descriptor Cards

Writer

As the writer, it will be your job to present a piece of something that you wrote and let your peers know what it is you are struggling with or what the goal is for your piece. Use the **Goals List** to help with your goal setting, the **Feedback Type Checklist** to help decide what type of feedback you want, and the **Identifying an Issue Checklist** to help determine what you need or want help with. Here are your feedback choices:

- Feedback on goals only

- Feedback on issues only

- Feedback on goals and issues

- "I heard . . ." feedback only

- No feedback (only available once)

Once you've told your peers what you want, summarize your piece briefly, and then read it aloud to them so that they can give helpful feedback based on what you asked for. When you are finished reading, call on one person at a time to give you feedback (if you wanted feedback), and use the **Writer Reflection Organizer** to take notes on. Later, you can decide what feedback you want to keep and what feedback you do not want before editing your piece.

Responder

As the responder, it will be your responsibility to pay attention to what the writer has asked for in feedback. You may use the **Peer Feedback Checklist** to write down what the writer asked for, and use the **Active Listening Checklist** to be sure you listen with close attention so you can give the most useful feedback possible. While the writer is reading, you can take notes on the **Peer Feedback Checklist** and then reflect after reading using the **Responder Reflection Organizer**. When you are called on by the writer, remember to first say something positive using an "I liked . . ." statement, followed with "I heard . . ." statements, before offering any feedback suggestions. Next, offer feedback focused on the writer's feedback choice. Remember: *Do not* use the word *you* in a statement unless it is a question or within the "I liked . . ." phrase.

Editor

As editor, it will be your responsibility to help the writer use helpful feedback in each peer-coaching session to make a better draft. You may use the **Editor's Before Coaching Checklist** for help in preparing the draft for the first peer-coaching session, the **Editor's After and Between Coaching Checklist** for using feedback from the first session to prepare writing for the next session, and the **Editor's Final Checklist** to help the writer prepare a final copy. In this responsibility, it will be important for you to keep track of and respond with what feedback the writer asked for, what the writer wanted help with, and what the goals are for the draft.

Manager

As manager, you will help organize and keep track of the peer-coaching session—a big responsibility! You may use the **Manager's Checklist** for this, checking off areas for the writer, responder, and editor. You are a coach in this role—remind your peers when they forget to use one of the protocols, such as in responding with an "I liked . . ." statement or staying away from using *you*. Also, make sure they stick to the type of feedback the writer asked for. Here are the feedback choices:

- Feedback on goals only
- Feedback on issues only
- Feedback on goals and issues
- "I heard . . ." feedback only
- No feedback (only available once)

If you aren't sure how this all works, being a manager is a nice opportunity to learn how. Pay attention, and good luck, manager!

31. Steps and Guidelines for Writer

Step One: Establish Goals and Issues, and Make a Feedback Choice

- Communicate your goals for the writing.
- Decide what issues you need help with.
- Select what type of feedback you want (see Feedback poster).

Step Two: Summarize and Read

- Summarize your writing in 1 minute or less.
- Read your piece aloud to the responder.

Step Three: Decide What Feedback to Use

- Take what you need (in feedback) and leave out what you do not.
- Make adjustments to your writing.

32. Steps and Guidelines for Responder

Step One: Listen for the Goals and Issues

- Listen carefully for what the writer says his/her goal is for the draft (take notes, ask questions).

- Listen carefully for what the writer says she or he needs help with in feedback on the issues. Ask clarifying questions when necessary.

Step Two: Listen to the Piece as It Is Read (Listening With a Purpose)

- Listen to provide feedback.
- Employ active listening.

Step Three: Give Feedback to the Writer

After listening to the writer read aloud, respond with feedback:

- First, say what you liked best using "I liked . . ." followed by "I heard . . ." statements.

- Next, offer feedback focused on what the writer asked for.

- Do not use the word *you* in a statement unless it is a question, or in an "I liked . . ." phrase.

33. Feedback Choices for Writer

1   I want feedback on my goals only.

2   I want feedback on my issues only.

3   I want feedback on my goals and issues.

4   I only want "I heard . . ." feedback on what my peer-coaching buddies heard in the draft.

5   No feedback—I just want to read aloud and be heard. (This option is only available once.)

34. List of Responsibilities for Editor

1 Provide helpful feedback to the writer before and after peer-coaching sessions.

2 Use the editor's checklists when helping the writer.
- Editor's Before Coaching Checklist
- Editor's After and Between Coaching Checklist
- Editor's Final Checklist

3 Keep track of the writer's goals and issues.

4 Keep track of feedback the writer asks for.

5 Help the writer use his or her feedback.

6 Provide the writer with helpful feedback for editing his or her piece.

35. List of Responsibilities for Manager

1 Help organize and keep track of peer-coaching sessions.

2 Use the Manager's Checklist to coach and help writer, responder, and editor in fulfilling their roles.

3 Use "I" statements, such as "I liked . . ." and "I might . . . ," when making suggestions to peers.

4 Offer assistance to others as needed in fulfilling roles successfully, to include using the proper forms and checklists.

36. Active Listening Checklist

❑ Give the speaker your undivided attention.

- Face your body toward the speaker, hands on your lap, ready to take notes.

❑ Pay attention to the speaker's body language—it will help you remember what was read.

- Often what is *not* said speaks louder.

❑ Don't give a distraction (a thought or noise) any more than 30 seconds of your time!

- Think about what the writer's goals and feedback request were to bring you back to "listening mode."
- It is impossible to listen and talk at the same time.

❑ Take mental pictures and think of summaries to lock information into memory.

❑ Ask questions when needed.

❑ Take notes during and after the reading.

❑ Reflect on the reading using the Responder Reflection Organizer *after* the reading.

❑ Use the Good Listening Rubric to see how you did after a listening session!

Conclusion

Helping Adolescent Writers
Find Their Voices

> *"That's a mountain. From now on that's a mountain. Got it?" Harriett looked up into his face. Sport moved back a pace. "Looks like an old tree root," he muttered. Harriett pushed her hair back and looked at him seriously. "Sport, what are you going to be when you grow up?" "You know what. You know I'm going to be a ball player." "Well, I'm going to be a writer. And when I say that's a mountain, that's a mountain."*
>
> —Louise Fitzhugh, *Harriett the Spy*

What began as an effort to meet the needs of my emerging student writers (and meet my own needs as a writer) blossomed into a process that I couldn't have anticipated. I certainly did not set out to create a method of student peer coaching. But I did set out to provide for students the minimum of what I needed as a writer: understanding, helpful feedback, and validation. Knowing what worked for me translated into exactly that for them. The rest was completely my students' doing. Like anything else creative, it took on a life of its own, and my young students had everything to do with it. Here is what Kate, one of my former middle school students, wrote to me recently:

> I think everyone has "that teacher" that really impacted their lives when they were in middle/high school. You were that teacher for me. I think often of how life might have been different . . . I'd probably still be petrified of public speaking. I don't know that I'd be in the job I'm in now. And I'm certain that I wouldn't blog my life for the world to see. I know for a fact that none of my creative writing would be up for anyone to read either! (Kate Moynihan, personal correspondence, October 15, 2008)

Kate, an educator in North Carolina, is in the process of teaching the students in her school the methods we used, methods that worked so well for her and many others: student peer coaching. Her kind words make me reflect back on my experiences in Miss Niblack's third-grade class, where I saw myself as a writer early on.

There are few absolutes when it comes to educating the minds of adolescents. But I can say with absolute certainty that if we allow students to write from inside of themselves, and be Who They Are without imposing on them Who We Are as writers, they *will* find their voices.

As teachers of adolescent writers, implement student peer coaching while mindful of the protocols that work to integrate themselves into students' academic abilities as they develop into better writers. Remember that these protocols aren't meant to be crutches—rather, they have been designed to help transition your students to that independent, inner, on-demand place where they can write, revise, edit, and ask for help as needed, whenever they need to, wherever they are. This is not just the essence of student peer coaching, but of any good teaching practice. Best wishes for fruitful implementation!

References

Atwell, N. (1998). *In the middle: New understandings about writing, reading, and learning* (2nd ed.). Portsmouth, NH: Boynton/Cook.

Atwell, N. (2007). Afterword. In K. Beers, R. E. Probst, & L. Rief (Eds.), *Adolescent literacy: Turning promise into practice* (pp. 311–314). Portsmouth, NH: Heinemann.

Beers, K., Probst, R. E., & Rief, L. (2007). *Adolescent literacy: Turning promise into practice.* Portsmouth, NH: Heinemann.

Calkins, L. M. (1983). *Lessons from a child: On the teaching and learning of writing.* Portsmouth, NH: Heinemann.

Elbow, P. (1973). *Writing without teachers.* New York: Oxford University Press.

Fletcher, R. J., & Portalupi, J. (2001). *Writing workshop: The essential guide.* Portsmouth, NH: Heinemann.

Graves, D. (1983). *Writing: Teachers and children at work.* Berkeley, CA: Heinemann.

Graves, D. H. (1994). *A fresh look at writing.* Portsmouth, NH: Heinemann.

Hawe, E., Dixon, H., & Watson, E. (2008). Oral feedback in the context of written language. *Australian Journal of Language and Literacy, 31*(1), 43–58.

Jensen, E. (2005). *Teaching with the brain in mind* (2nd ed.). Alexandria, VA: Association for Supervision and Curriculum Development.

Kirby, D., Kirby, D., & Liner, T. (2004). *Inside out: Strategies for teaching writing* (3rd ed.). Portsmouth, NH: Heinemann.

Moran, P. P., & Greenberg, B. (2008). Peer revision: Helping students to develop a meta-editor. *Ohio Journal of English Language Arts, 48,* 33–39.

Murray, D. M. (1985). *A writer teaches writing* (2nd ed.). Boston: Houghton Mifflin.

Robb, L. (1998). *Easy-to-manage reading & writing conferences.* New York: Scholastic.

Simmons, J. (2003). Responders are taught, not born: Research in four high school writing classes demonstrated that these college bound students need several years of experience to develop the ability to respond helpfully to peer writing. *Journal of Adolescent & Adult Literacy, 45*(8), 684–693.

Tomlinson, C. A. (2003). *Fulfilling the promise of the differentiated classroom.* Alexandria, VA: Association for Supervision and Curriculum Development.

Vacca, R. T., & Vacca, J. L. (2005). *Content area reading: Literacy and learning across the curriculum* (8th ed.). Boston: Pearson Custom.

Wiggins, G. P., & McTighe, J. (1998). *Understanding by design.* Alexandria, VA: Association for Supervision and Curriculum Development.

Wolfe, P. (2001). *Brain matters: Translating research into classroom practice.* Alexandria, VA: Association for Supervision and Curriculum Development.

Index